Duncan J. D. Smith

ONLY IN TANGIER

A Guide to Unique Locations,
Hidden Corners and Unusual Objects

Photographs by
Duncan J. D. Smith
except where stated otherwise

Top left: Weaver Douae La Hrir at Dar al-Drazz on Rue Ibn Abbou (Kasbah) (see no. 25)
Top right: Woodworker Abdul Latif Kasabji on Rue Amrah (Medina) (see no. 13)
Bottom left: A communal bakery at the corner of Rue Oudrass and Rue Cheikh Mohamed Ben Seddik (Medina) (see no. 10)
Bottom right: A date and fig seller on Rue d'Italie (Ville Nouvelle) (see no. 1)

Contents

Introduction

"Hemmed with hills, confronted by the sea, and looking like a white cape draped on the shores of Africa, it is an international city with an excellent climate."

Truman Capote, *The Dogs Bark* (1973)

The Moroccan port city of Tangier (Arabic *Tanjah*) is a liminal place. A conduit between Europe and Africa, it overlooks the Strait of Gibraltar, where the Atlantic meets the Mediterranean. With Spain just nine miles away, it has long been a magnet for colonists, refugees, and creatives, a place where, as Moroccan novelist Mohamed Choukri (1935–2003) declared, "everything is surreal and everything is possible". These days it is as much a stepping-off point for migrants heading north as it is for visitors lured south by a sense of adventure. This multicultural fusion makes Tangier a city unique in Morocco.

The strategic importance of Tangier determined its historical destiny. Its story began around 10,000 BC when white-skinned hunters arrived from the Iberian Peninsula and bred with immigrants from the Near East to produce the Berber (more correctly Amazigh) people of Morocco's Rif Mountains. By 1500 BC Phoenician traders had appeared from the Levant, followed in the 5th century BC by the Carthaginians who kick-started the city's long colonial history by establishing the trading post of Tingis.

The fall of Carthage in 146 BC brought the Romans who, in 82 BC, annexed Tingis as Colonia Iulia Tingi. In 25 BC, the Berber kings of northern Morocco became the Romans' vassals and in AD 40 the last Berber king, Ptolemy of Mauretania (c. 13 BC–AD 40), was executed to curtail Berber autonomy. Two years later the area was split into two Roman provinces, Tingis becoming part of the province of Mauretania Tingitana.

By AD 285, Rome had abandoned its North African ambitions although the region remained a part of the Roman Empire until 429, when the Vandals attacked from Spain. They were ousted in 534 by the Byzantines. By 698, most of North Africa had been taken by the Arab forces of the Umayyad Caliphate who converted the Berbers to Islam. This triggered a long succession of Muslim Berber dynasties – from the Idrisids (788–974) to the Saadians (1544–1659) – who ruled from Fes and Marrakesh.

Tangier was a special case. It remained a small settlement until 1471, when it was taken by the Portuguese King Alfonso V (1432–1481). He strengthened the existing walled Medina (Old City) in order to keep other Europeans out of North Africa. In 1661, it passed to the British, who received it as the dowry of Catherine of Braganza (1638–1705), sister of the king of Portugal, when she married Charles II (1630–1685). They relinquished it to Morocco and the Sunni Alawi Sultanate in 1684.

A period of relative regional stability followed until 1830 when France invaded Algeria. The threat of further European encroachment culminated in 1912 when Morocco became a French protectorate. Again Tangier was an exception. The Paris Convention of December 1923, which ultimately came into force in June 1925, resulted in Tangier being governed by an international commission. Between 1925 and Moroccan independence in 1956 it remained an International Zone and Free Port administered by representatives of the thirteen victors of the Great War. Dubbed the Interzone by writer William Burroughs (1914–1997), this short and often licentious chapter has unfairly overshadowed what came before and after, a fact only enhanced by the intrigues of the Second World War.

Since 1957, the Alawi sultans have ruled Morocco as kings. Whereas Hassan II (1929–1999) distrusted Tangier for its association with foreigners, his son Mohammed VI (b. 1963) has invested heavily in upgrading the city's infrastructure, including a revived waterfront, sanitised Medina, new cargo port, and high-speed rail link to Casablanca.

Only in Tangier has been written for independent cultural travellers. This is the Tangier of old forts and new mosques, historic hotels and contemporary gardens, traditional crafts and modern art. The fifty-five locations represent the author's personal odyssey through the city and beyond, which together showcase its famous and less well-known sights.

Tangier is not divided strictly into administrative zones. Instead, it consists of long-established districts and more recent suburbs. Most visitors head straight for the Medina in the northeast corner of the city. Its labyrinthine alleys and flat-roofed, whitewashed buildings climb uphill through four distinct neighbourhoods – Beni Idder, Oued Aherdane, Yenan Kaptan, and Dar Baroud – to the separately fortified Kasbah palace at the top.

The Ville Nouvelle (New City), which represents the 20th-century expansion of Tangier southwards, is no less interesting for its European-style architecture, entertainment venues, and artistic connections. The well-to-do inner suburbs of Tangier include the Marshan, Iberia (San Francisco), Old Mountain, and New Mountain (California), with their Colonial-era homes, apartment of writer Paul Bowles (1910–1999), and British pet cemetery. The outer suburbs of Rmilat and Achakkar to the west, Ziaten to the south, and Malabata to the east have their gardens and the Caves of Hercules, top-notch sporting facilities, and leisurely beach life respectively. Farther afield is the old fortified town of Asilah, blue-painted Chefchaouen, and Tétouan in the lee of the Rif Mountains.

Walking is the best way to get around, with taxis and buses for the suburbs and beyond. So, whether shopping at the Central Market, savouring a view enjoyed by the artist Matisse, people-watching on the Petit Socco, or looking for the tomb of medieval traveller Ibn Battouta, *Only in Tangier* will encourage readers to set out on their own urban expedition.

1 Shopping at the Central Market

Medina (Old City), the Central Market (Marché Central) on Rue Siaghine (note: be sure to ask stallholders for their permission before taking photographs)

Tangier offers a wide assortment of food shops to satisfy the needs of its denizens. Daily shopping is done by many in independent grocery stores known as *hanouts*. This Maghrebi Arabic word lends itself to *Ras el Hanout* ('top shelf') which signifies the best in-house spice mix a shop can offer. Generic by comparison are the supermarket chains, notably Carrefour and Marjane, and the Ibn Battouta and Malabata Malls. For visitors, however, the most memorable shopping experience will be a visit to the Central Market (Marché Central).

The location of the market is telling. Built up against the wall of the Medina (Old City) in the late-19th century, it is reached through a gate called Bab Fondaq Zraa. The name recalls the caravanserais *(fondouks)* of old, once situated hereabouts, where visiting merchants stored their wares and rested overnight. In time, these caravanserais morphed into a permanent outdoor market, the Grand Socco, which in turn was replaced by the covered Central Market seen today (see no. 18). The building's iron framework is original.

Stretching southwards along the Rue de la Plage, the market consists of a series of halls where vivid colours,

A colourful fruit stall inside the Central Market

pungent smells, and lively conversation assault the senses. There are stalls selling herbs and brightly-coloured spices, dried figs and dates, nuts, vegetables, couscous, and lamb, all staples of the Moroccan diet. There is plenty of bread, cheese, and eggs, too. The fruit inevitably includes tangerines, a mandarin-type orange grown in the Tangier region and exported from the 18th century onwards (the natives of Tangier are known variously as tangerines or more commonly *tanjawis*). There are also mountains of olives, which is hardly surprising since Morocco is one of the world's largest growers of olives, with groves covering more than 1,214,000 hectares (3 million acres). They are available in a bewildering array of sizes and colours from the wild, dark-brown *Bouzoug* variety to the large, cultivated green *Manzanilla* type. A dozen or more varieties alone are grown and harvested for oil.

At the far end of the market there is a separate fish hall (Marché Central de Poissons). A visit here is a truly local experience, with all sorts of fish and other sea creatures laid out on stone slabs for the scrutiny of restaurateurs and private individuals alike. Plans to modernise the Central Market will most likely result in a loss of this sort of character.

Immediately outside the market along Rue de la Plage and Rue d'Italie are other stalls selling more herbs and spices, dried fruits, coffee, and household items (see page 2). On Tuesdays, Thursdays, and Sundays Jebala women from the western Rif Mountains set up makeshift pavement stalls on these streets (and on Rue Tijania inside the Medina, too). Identified by their colourful pompomed straw hats, they peddle seasonal fresh fruit and vegetables, fragrant bunches of mint and coriander, and fresh goat cheese *(jben)* wrapped in palm fronds. The latter is delicious on a piece of freshly-baked circular flatbread *(chubz/msemmen)*.

There are some interesting suburban markets in Tangier, too. The Casa Barata, for example, on Avenue Abou el Kacem Acharif Sebti is a large, covered market noted for its *melée* of tradespeople, including blacksmiths, carpenters, fabric merchants, pan sellers, and carpet dealers. Outside is a huge fruit and vegetable market. The Souk Dradeb on Rocade Dradeb is a haven for shoppers who wish to buy their groceries direct from local suppliers. Certainly the chickens roaming free are not something one sees in a modern supermarket!

Other locations nearby: 2, 3, 5, 18, 19, 20

2 The Sweetest Treats

Medina (Old City), some sweet shops and patisseries including Nougat de Tangier at the junction of Rue Siaghine and Rue Synagogues

Moroccans certainly have a sweet tooth. Sweet shops and patisseries abound in Tangier serving all manner of treats, many with a Middle Eastern origin. What follows is a whistlestop tasting tour of a few of them.

At the junction of Rue Siaghine and Rue Synagogues in the Medina (Old City) there stands the oldest public fountain *(saqiyah)* in Tangier. Alongside it is a modest retail kiosk that, since 1952, has been dispensing arguably the best artisanal nougat. Chewy and not overly sweet, it is still made by the same family from a paste of creamy honey and beaten egg whites combined with roasted nuts (hazelnuts, pistachios, and almonds) and chopped dried fruit. The result is known as white nougat to distinguish it from brown nougat, which is made without egg whites and has a firmer, often crunchy texture.

One of the earliest recipes for white nougat appears in a 10th century book written in Baghdad. It states that *natif*, as nougat was first known, originated in the city of Harran in south-east Turkey, close by the Syrian border. From there it spread to Spain and Italy during the 15th century, and then to France two centuries later. The word 'nougat' derives from the Southern European *Occitan* word *nogat* meaning 'nutty'.

Nougat de Tangier on Rue Siaghine

Moroccan sweets at Chez Hassan on Rue de la Kasbah

There are, of course, other places selling good nougat in Tangier. They include Nougat del Norte also on Rue Siaghine at number 13, and Nougat el Awami Tanger outside the Medina on Avenue Belgique (Ville Nouvelle). There are plenty of good patisseries, too, selling a wide range of sweets, cakes, and biscuits. One of them is Al-Moutamid Bnou Abbad which is tucked away at 16 Rue Mouatimid Ben Abbad (Ville Nouvelle). With more than 30 traditional Moroccan pastries to choose from, this is the place to visit for your almond-filled Gazelle Horns *(Kaab el Gazal)*, doughnuts *(sfenj)*, cinnamon-laced shortbread *(ghriba)*, *chebakia* coated in honey, orangle blossom syrup, and sesame seeds, chocolate-covered *merendina* sponge, and curly, almond-filled *mencha*. No less Moroccan are semolina bread *(harcha)*, semolina pancakes *(baghir)*, and circular flatbreads *(msemmen)*. Do not be put off by the shop's modest exterior. Inside is a riot of colourful *zellij* tiles set off against a beautifully carved wooden ceiling.

Other patisseries in the New City (Ville Nouvelle) include Al Andalous at 101 Rue de la Liberté, Café La Española on the same street at number 97, and Matisse on Rue Allal Ben Abdellah.

A couple of streets north of Rue Siaghine are some traditional Moroccan residences known as *riads*. Anonymous from the outside but with inner courtyards decorated with tiles *(zellij)*, fountains, and potted plants for coolness, such buildings first appeared during the Idrisid Dynasty (788–974 AD). Those now used for visitor accommodation include Riad Tingis on Rue Nejjarine, Dar Nakhla Naciria on Rue Naciria, Riad Amr on Rue Lokous, and Riad Arous Chamel on Rue Ben Abdessadak.

Other locations nearby: 1, 3, 4, 5, 6, 18

3 The Jews of Tangier

Medina (Old City), a Jewish history tour including the Moshe Nahon Synagogue at the end of Rue Cheikh al Harrak, a cul-de-sac off Rue Synagogues

Stucco and stained glass at the Moshe Nahon Synagogue

The Jews have a long history in Morocco stretching back at least 1,700 years. During this time, their community waxed and waned from a population high of around 300,000 during the 1950s (the largest in the Muslim world) to barely 2,300 today. In Tangier, a community that once boasted as many as 27,000 members and 17 synagogues has been reduced to less than 100 souls and a single functioning place of worship.

The earliest evidence of Judaism in Morocco dates from the Roman period in the form of Hebrew gravestones of the 3rd century. With the adoption of Christianity by the Romans, the Jews were officially persecuted. Following the Arab conquest of north-west Africa during the early 8th century, the Jews experienced mixed fortunes at the hands of a succession of dynasties.

The Spanish and Portuguese expulsion of Jews in 1492 and 1496 respectively saw a great influx of Sephardic Jews into Morocco. Known as *megorashim*, these new arrivals contributed to the rise of the Fez-Meknes-based Alawi Dynasty (1631–present) for whom they acted as merchants, bankers, and ambassadors. By the 19th century, burgeoning European colonialism favoured north Moroccan ports, especially Tangier, where the Jewish community became well established. However, persecution and scapegoating persisted in the fragmented Sultanate, and the creation in 1912 of a French Protectorate over most of Morocco encouraged Moroccans to improve their own lives sometimes at the cost of the Jews. With the emergence of Zionism and the creation of Israel in 1948, more than 275,000 Jews swapped Morocco for Israel, where today almost five million Jews of Moroccan descent are living. When Morocco gained independence in 1956, those Jews remaining were accorded citizenship on a par with Muslims.

The old Jewish Quarter of Tangier can be found in the Beni Idder neighbourhood in the southern part of the Medina. Unlike other cities, where Jews were contained in a walled and gated *mellah*, the Jews of Tangier blended freely with their Muslim neighbours. Two of their once-numerous synagogues still stand along the aptly-named Rue Synagogues, which runs south off Rue Siaghine ('Silversmiths' Street' since the Jews traded silver here). The modest Akiva Laredo Synagogue dates from the mid-19th century, its name echoing its builder's Spanish origin. Farther along, at the end of Rue Cheikh al Harrak, a cul-de-sac running off Rue Synagogues, is the Moshe Nahon Synagogue. It was commissioned in 1878 by Moshe Nahon, a prominent Jewish banker and scholar who was also responsible for Tangier's first department store, the Magasins Modernes at 91 Rue Siaghine. The synagogue's main sanctuary is decorated beautifully in Andalusian style, with stuccoed walls, stained glass, ornate silver lanterns, and gold-embroidered curtains concealing the *Torah* scrolls that were read from the raised lectern *(bimah)* nearby. The upstairs gallery was originally the women's prayer area *(hazara)*. A third synagogue, named for Rabbi Mordechai Bengio, stands around the corner at 44 Rue Touahine. Built in 1880, it today houses the Musée-Fondation Lorin, a performance space and collection of photos, paintings, posters, and maps illustrating 20th century Tangier.

Beyond the wall of the Medina, which runs along Rue du Portugal, lies a sprawling Jewish Cemetery. It contains more than a thousand headstones, some dating back to the 16th century. After its closure in 1910, Jewish burials were made in a new cemetery on Avenue Moulay Abdelaziz to the south.

The only functioning synagogue left in Tangier is housed in a former villa at 27 Boulevard Pasteur (Ville Nouvelle). Completed in 1919, the building was converted into the Chaar Rafael synagogue in 1954, when the owner Raphaël Bendriahm died.

Other locations nearby: 1, 2, 4, 5, 6

4 The American Legation Museum

Medina (Old City), the Tangier American Legation Museum at 8 Rue d'Amerique (note: the museum website uses the post-colonial address 8 Zankat Amrika)

In 1684, the British abandoned their colony in Tangier, worn down by years of Berber attacks and escalating costs. This left Morocco in the hands of the Alawi Sultanate. Although the following decades saw periods of regional disarray, the country was eventually unified under Sultan Mohammed ibn Abdallah (1710–1790), who is remembered as "the architect of modern Morocco". It was he who first invited various European powers to establish consulates in Tangier, which became the country's diplomatic capital.

Until the construction of purpose-built headquarters during the 20th century, foreign consuls occupied old houses in the Medina. By 1830, Denmark, France, Great Britain, Portugal, Sardinia, Spain, Sweden, and Tuscany all had consuls based in Tangier. The French Consulate, for example, was housed in a Portuguese-era building at 41 Rue Siaghine (see no. 5). Another interesting consular presence in the city was the Old American Legation at 8 Rue d'Amerique.

On 20th December 1777, Morocco became the first nation to recognise American independence from Great Britain. This was facilitated through the sultan's dealings with the Spanish Governer of Louisiana, Luis de Unzaga (1717–1793), a man whose keen nose for commer-

A corner of the Tangier American Legation Museum

cial opportunities earned him the moniker 'le Concilateur'. The Treaty of Peace and Friendship signed between the two countries in 1787 remains the longest unbroken agreement between the United States and a foreign nation. In return, in 1821, Sultan Sulayman bin Mohammed (1766–1822) donated a small palace to the United States' government for use as a diplomatic mission. It was the first property acquired abroad by the United States. Enlarged in 1926, it fulfilled its function for 140 years before being closed in 1961 following Moroccan independence (thereafter, the capital city of Rabat became Morocco's diplomatic centre).

The Old American Legation today is the only building outside the United States to be on the American Registry of Historic Places. In 1976, private donations facilitated the creation of a foundation that transformed the then largely-abandoned building into a museum, gallery, library, and cultural community centre. The museum contains documents and artefacts relating to the American diplomatic presence in Tangier, the various consuls, and the famous Americans who spent time in the city, including William Burroughs (1914–1997), Tennessee Williams (1911–1983), and Truman Capote (1924–1984). Two rooms are dedicated to the writer and composer Paul Bowles (1910–1999), who spent half a century in Tangier (see no. 38). On display are his typewriters, first edition books, musical scores, folk music recordings, and a stack of well-travelled suitcases.

The museum also contains a collection of works by artists who lived in or passed through Tangier, including the Frenchmen Eugene Delacroix (1798–1863) and Henri Matisse (1869–1954), the Austrian Oskar Kokoschka (1886–1980), and the Scotsman James McBey (1883–1959), whose wife Marguerite (1905–1999) was instrumental in forming the collection (see nos. 23, 40). Moroccan art is represented by the works of Mohammed Hamri (1932–2000) and Mohammed Ben Ali R'bati (1861–1939).

Near to the Old American Legation are two *marabouts*. A dozen of these tombs-turned-shrines of Muslim holy men are in the Medina. The Marabout Sidi Amar Aliech is immediately next door and can be identied by its gated, horseshoe-shaped entrance. Aliech, a singing Riffian saint, who claimed to foretell the future, lived and died in a house here. The second *marabout*, on Place Taqaddum, marks the former home of the powerful Sharif of Ouezzane, Sidi Abdeslam (1834–1892), who was considered a direct descendant of the Prophet (see no. 21).

Other locations nearby: 1, 2, 3, 5, 6

5 Home of the Sultan's Agent

Medina (Old City), the Dar Niaba Museum (Musée Dar Niaba) at 41 Rue Siaghine

On Rue Siaghine (Medina), alongside the Church of the Immaculate Conception, there stands a battered monumental doorway. Finely carved with Classical-style half-columns, it represents the only tangible evidence of Portuguese-era Tangier (1471–1661) other than the city walls (see no. 12). Presumably originally part of a mansion or palace, from 1816 onwards it gave access to the French Consulate.

By 1830, several European countries including France and Great Britain, had official representatives based in Tangier. Their job was to assist and protect their country's citizens, including merchants, diplomats, engineers, and military men, and to facilitate trade relations with Morocco. During the mid-1840s, with commercial activity on the increase, Sultan Abd al-Rahman (1778–1859) appointed a trusted, permanent deputy in Tangier through which his government *(Makhzen)* could not only liaise with these consuls but also limit their activities if necessary. This man was known as the *Naib*.

In 1849, the French Consulate relocated and the old building with the eyecatching doorway was sold back to the Moroccan government. As a result, from 1851 onwards it became the administrative headquarters of the *Naib*. Known as Dar Niaba (House of the Naib), this is where five of the seven successive *Naibs* were based. The first two were based outside Tangier since initially the office of *Naib* was combined with ter-

The peaceful inner courtyard of the Dar Niaba Museum

ritorial authority elsewhere. From 1851 onwards, however, the role of *Naib* came without territorial authority and Tangier became the geographical preserve of a Governor *(Pasha)* based in the Kasbah Palace at the top of the Medina (see no. 17). The fifth *Naib*, Mohammed Torres (1820–1908), was also Moroccan foreign minister. He was present at the 1906 Algeciras Conference, which confirmed French pre-eminence among the European powers in Morocco at the time.

Following the Treaty of Fez (1912) by the terms of which most of Morocco became a French protectorate, the office of *Naib* continued as a symbolic role only. The last *Naib* was Mohammed Tazi (d. 1954), who fulfilled the role between 1913 and 1925, when Tangier was declared an International Zone and the role of *Naib* was replaced by that of *Mendoub*. It was this man's job to administer the affairs of the Muslim and Jewish communities, which together comprised most of Tangier's inhabitants. Mohammed Tazi also served as the first *Mendoub*, remaining in the new position until his death in 1954. With Moroccan independence in 1956, the office of *Mendoub* became redundant.

In 1920, in the wake of the Treaty of Versailles, a building formerly used by the German Legation near the Grand Socco had been repurposed as the ceremonial headquarters of the *Mendoub* (see no. 19). The old Dar Niaba on Rue Siaghine subsequently became municipal offices and was eventually abandoned. Not until the early-2020s was it renovated and in 2022 it opened to the public as the Dar Niaba Museum (Musée Dar Niaba). Beyond the monumental stone doorway, today's visitors will find a tranquil orange tree-filled courtyard and a modest collection of documents and artefacts illustrating the diplomatic history of Tangier since the 18th century. There is also a gallery of Moroccan-themed artworks assembled from various local private collections. These include several terracotta figurines of Moroccans made by the Austrian ceramicist Johann Maresch (1821–1914) and a collection of Moroccan portrait paintings by the Spanish Orientalist artist Diego Marin Lopes (1865–1917). In the courtyard are some accomplished landscape scenes rendered in Andalusian-style ceramics.

Other locations nearby: 1, 2, 3, 4, 6

6 People-watching on the Petit Socco

Medina (Old City), a stroll around the Petit Socco

Everyone in Tangier eventually finds themselves in the Petit Socco. Located in the southern (lower) part of the Medina, this elongated square has been a social and commercial hub for over 2,000 years. It is best reached from the Grand Socco by means of Rue Siaghine, the Medina's main west–east axis, which separates the neighbourhoods of Beni Idder and Oued Aherdane.

The name 'Petit Socco' (sometimes Soco Chico) encapsulates the city's French and Spanish legacy. *Socco* is the north Moroccan rendering of the Spanish *zoco*, itself a corruption of the Arabic *souk* meaning market. Whatever the spelling, the meaning is the same: little market. The square's official name is Place Souk Dakhil (Square of the Inner Souk) to distinguish it from the Grand Socco outside the Medina (see no. 18).

Early evening in the Petit Socco

During Roman times, the Petit Socco was the site of the Forum and so a hub for commercial affairs (see no. 33). A market no doubt existed on the same spot during the Portuguese era. Old maps clearly show caravanserais *(fondouks)* located outside the main gate (Bab al-Fahs) at the top end of Rue Siaghine, where goods would be offloaded and stored before being brought down to the Petit Socco for sale. Visiting sailors would walk up to the

Petit Socco from the Port by means of the Bab el-Marsa (Harbour Gate) and Rue de la Marine.

During the 19th and early-20th centuries Europeans built the Ville Nouvelle (New City) outside the walls of the Medina and with it came bigger market facilities. The old market on the Petit Socco was gradually broken up, with traders relocating around the corner onto Rue Almohades. In their place came new enterprises such as banks, post offices, hotels, and cafés. By the time of the Tangier International Zone (1925–1956) each of the controlling foreign powers, as well as Morocco, had its own bank, currency, and post office. A good example is the Hispano-Moorish style building standing at the east end of the Petit Socco at 76 Rue de la Marine. This building was home to a branch of the Banque d'Etat du Maroc, forerunner of the present day Bank al-Maghrib, until 1952 when it moved to a new and larger facility on Avenue Mohamed V (Ville Nouvelle). Today, the building houses the glamorous Restaurant Palais Zahi and it is well worth a peep inside.

Another International Zone-era structure is the triangular-arched former Spanish Post and Telegraph Office on Rue des Postes. Completed in 1926, it was the first *Art Deco* building in Tangier. Following Moroccan independence in 1956, it became the Casa Nazareth, a home for poor Spaniards run by the Spanish Franciscan Brothers of Cruz Blanca. Today they care for disabled Moroccans and street minors.

An ages-old activity in the Petit Socco is people-watching. The cafés all have their outside seats with their backs to the wall to facilitate this habit. Over the course of a day all types have passed this way from the errand-boys and money changers of old to today's street entertainers and tour guides. It is said that spending time here is the best way to understand the Tanjawi soul. The venerable Café Tingis (with its vintage French–Spanish signboard) and Café Central at the top end of the square are good spots for this, as is the balcony of the Hotel Fuentes. William Burroughs (1914–1997) gained inspiration for his book *The Naked Lunch* (1959) on the terrace of the Central. A little later Truman Capote (1924–1984) described the atmosphere, habitués, and "hurdy gurdy clamour" of the Petit Socco in his book *The Dogs Bark* (1973).

Other locations nearby: 2, 3, 4, 5, 7, 8

7 Music at the Gnawa House

Medina (Old City), the Dar Gnawa in lock-up number 2 in the Borj el-Hajoui courtyard on Rue Alkaa just inside the Bab el-Marsa (note: unfortunately there are no fixed opening hours)

One of the main gates on the seaward side of the Medina (Old City) is the Bab el-Marsa. Its name means 'Harbour Gate' since it was originally used by visiting sailors to reach the Petit Socco. These days if you pass through it you might be fortunate and hear music in the air. This is *gnawa*, a fusion of pre-Islamic West African music with Moroccan rhythms, and it is coming from an unmarked lock-up in a courtyard on Rue Alkaa.

Gnawa emerged during the 16th and 17th centuries, when West Africans, notably from the Hausa, Fulani, and Bambara peoples in the Sahel, were brought to Morocco as slaves (the word *gnawa* used to describe them probably derives from 'Kano', a city in northern Nigeria). During the reign of Sultan Ismail Ibn Sharif (1645–1727) these slaves were formed into a loyal military corps called the Black Guard. Indoctrinated with the works of the Persian Sunni scholar Muhammad al-Bukhari (810–870), they helped the sultan extend his authority over Morocco. When the French abolished slavery in Morocco in 1923, the *gnawa* became part of the Islamic Sufi order in the Maghreb.

Musician Abdellah El Gourd at the Dar Gnawa

Originally, the *gnawa* observed a complex all-night ceremony (*lila* or *derdeba*) consisting of ritualistic songs and dances to expel evil spirits *(djinn)* from the sick and to gain redemption from sin. Performed under the guidance of a *gnawa* master musician *(maâlem)* and a clairvoyant *(moqadma)*, these ceremonies evoked seven saints *(sidi)* and spirits *(mlouk)* through the repetition of chants that took several hours. The vocals were closely mimicked by a three-stringed fretless lute (*hejhouj*, *guembri* or *sintir*) accompanied by large iron castanets *(qraqab)*. Once in a state of possession *(jedba)*, the celebrants entered a trance and danced ecstatically.

In more recent times, the *gnawa* heritage in Morocco has become more profane. International musicians, including Robert Plant of Led Zeppelin (b. 1948) and Carlos Santana (b. 1947), have worked with *gnawa* musicians, and an annual *gnawa* festival is staged in the coastal town of Essaouira. In 2019, *gnawa* was inscribed on the Representative List of the Intangible Cultural Heritage of Humanity. It was in Tangier, however, that the campaign to preserve and promote *gnawa* began. During the 1960s, *gnawa* musicians began gathering at the home of *gnawa* maestro Abdellah El Gourd (b. 1947). They used the ground floor for live *gnawa* performances and improvised jam sessions. As such, the so-called Dar Gnawa became the first officially recognized centre devoted to celebrating and preserving the music of the descendants of slaves in Morocco. Indeed, for many years it was the only venue in the country where Moroccans could come to hear and play *gnawa*.

In 1992, El Gourd famously collaborated with American jazz pianist Randy Weston (1926–2018) on the Grammy-nominated album *The Splendid Master Gnawa Musicians of Morocco*. In 2021, however, his home in the Medina was declared unsafe. As a result, the Dar Gnawa relocated to lock-up number 2 in the Borj el-Hajoui courtyard on Rue Alkaa (the courtyard is easy to locate because it contains a pair of 19th century cannons; see no. 12). El Gourd still plays here intermittently surrounded by all manner of musical memorabilia from his long career. Performance times are erratic though so to enjoy the hypnotic thrum of *gnawa* one can always head over to YouTube. Alternatively, *gnawa* street musicians can sometimes be heard on the viewing terrace overlooking the courtyard.

Gnawa **includes Andalusian influences, too. To hear Andalusian music visit Les Fils du Détroit, a café-cum-performance space in a corner of Place du Kasbah, where musicians play 12-string ouds, flutes, and tambourines for the price of a mint tea.**

Other locations nearby: 5, 6, 9, 10

8 The Grand Mosque

Medina (Old City), the Grand Mosque (Jami' al-Kebir) at 76 Rue de la Marine (note: this is a working mosque and so closed to non-Muslims)

The Grand Mosque (Jami' al-Kebir) at 76 Rue de la Marine (Medina) is Tangier's historic main mosque (in Tangier the word *jami'* is used to describe a mosque rather than the more usual Arabic *masjid*). Although the current structure dates only from the early-19th century, it occupies a site that has seen a succession of religious buildings since antiquity.

The entrance and minaret of the Grand Mosque

Historians tell us that in Roman times a temple dedicated to Hercules stood here. Later, during the 5th century, this was replaced by a Roman church. The first Grand Mosque was built during the time of the Berber Marinid Dynasty, which controlled Morocco between the mid-13th and the 15th centuries. The mosque's proximity to what was then the Medina's main market (today's Petit Socco) followed that of the Roman temple and Forum, with both arrangements reflecting the traditional connection between commercial and religious life.

With the arrival of the Portuguese in 1471, the mosque was pressed into service as a cathedral. Not until the return of Tangier to Muslim rule in 1684 did the building revert to being a mosque. By this time, however, the mosque was far from being grand. Indeed in 1815 Sultan Sulayman bin Mohammed (1766–1822) was so shocked by its condition that he ordered it to be rebuilt. Completed in 1818, it was kept in good order this time as an enduring symbol of Islamic orthodoxy and a means to counter the growing popularity of Sufi brotherhoods in the city (see no. 14).

By the early years of the 20th century, the Ville Nouvelle (New City) was taking shape outside the walled Medina. As a result, the Grand Mosque's civic importance dwindled, especially following the emergence of the Tangier International Zone in 1925, when the machinery of government moved away from the Medina. This, however, did not stop Sultan Mohammed V (1909–1961) from using the mosque in 1947 as a pulpit from which to issue a clarion call for Moroccan independence (see no. 19).

The exterior of the mosque is distinguished by its ornate minaret and main door. The minaret is of traditional Moroccan form consisting of a tall, four-sided tower with merlons, topped off with a smaller tower. The outer walls are decorated with blind arches outlined in white stucco, infilled with either emerald green or polychrome ceramic tiles. The same green tiles, common to many Moroccan sacred structures because of their association with paradise and fertility, cover the roofs and surround the main door.

The interior consists of a square courtyard, open to the sky, with a central fountain. This is surrounded left and right by covered galleries, with the main prayer hall straight ahead, three aisles deep, each aisle separated by a columned arcade. At one end of the prayer hall is a niche *(mihrab)* that represents the Mecca-facing direction of prayer *(qibla)*.

In the past, several ancillary buildings were attached to the mosque. These included the imam's chamber, a library, and a funeral mosque for conducting pre-burial rites. On the street outside stood the house of the prayer timekeeper *(muwaqqit)*, the house of the judge *(qadi)*, the city's first Qur'anic school *(madrassa)*, and a hospital *(maristan)*. Still extant is a late-19th century, horseshoe-shaped public fountain *(saqiyah)* decorated with *zellij* tilework.

Several streets away on Rue Jamae stands the New Mosque (Jami' Jedida). Founded by Sultan Sulayman at the same time he ordered the Grand Mosque be rebuilt, it features an eyecatching red brick minaret again with green-tiled decoration. The name of nearby Rue du Palmier recalls a palm tree that almost matched the minaret in height.

Other locations nearby: 6, 7, 9, 13

9 The Historic Hotel Continental

Medina (Old City), the Hotel Continental at 36 Rue Dar Baroud (note: the hotel is closed currently pending sale to a new owner)

Given Tangier's colonial history and enduring popularity as a visitor destination, it is little wonder that it has become adept at providing guest accommodation. Notably, some of the city's old hotels have become legends for the guests they have hosted and the events they have witnessed. Chief among them is the Hotel Continental.

Located in the north-east corner of the Medina, the Hotel Continental was founded in the 1860s by the Ben Dahans, an old Jewish family from Spain, who represented the Ford Motor Company in Morocco. Its situation was ideal back in the days when passenger liners carrying over-wintering Europeans docked at the port below. Even before then the site was an important one. The car park in front of the hotel, for example, occupies the Borj al-Salam, a sturdy bastion that originally formed a part of the Portuguese-era walls protecting the Medina; a palace of the Sharif of Ouezzane, Sidi Abdeslam (1834–1892), was also located here (see nos. 12, 21).

In many ways the Hotel Continental remains the quintessential Colonial-era hotel despite its bedrooms having been upgraded. Its public areas still smack of the past, with their comfortable fusion of staid European and colourful Oriental design. The fireplace is smoke-

The Hotel Continental with the old Customs House in front

stained, there is a wind-up gramophone in the dining room, a 1930s-era telephone switchboard, a mosaic-tiled café, and a long-case clock on the main staircase that ticks lugubriously. No wonder the film director Bernardo Bertolucci (1941–2018) chose the Continental as the backdrop for some early scenes in his 1990 film *The Sheltering Sky* set in the late-1940s and based on a novel by the Tangier-based author Paul Bowles (1910–1999) (see no. 38). Photos of Bertolucci as well as John Malkovich (b. 1953), the film's leading man, hang on the wall.

The yellowing pages of the hotel's visitors' book contain the names of many notable guests: Winston Churchill (1874–1965); artist Edgar Degas (1834–1917) and architect Antonio Gaudí (1852–1926); actresses Greta Garbo (1905–1990) and Mary Pickford (1892–1979); Spanish novelist Pío Baroja (1872–1956); and President of the First Spanish Republic, Emilio Castelar (1832–1899). Another celebrated guest was HRH Prince Alfred, Duke of Edinburgh (1844–1900), who stayed at the hotel in 1884 and again in 1888. His coat of arms still adorns the entrance hall and his room is kept much as it was at the time.

Another hotel with history is the El Minzah, which opened in 1930 at 85 Rue de la Liberté (Ville Nouvelle), formerly the site of the townhouse of American lawyer Ion Hanford Perdicaris (1840–1925) who in May 1904 was famously kidnapped and held for ransom by Moroccan brigand, Ahmed ibn-Muhammed Raisuli (see no. 42). The El Minzah was built by the wealthy John Crichton-Stuart, Fourth Marquis of Bute (1881–1947), who had real estate interests in Tangier during the time of the International Zone (1925–1956). The hotel proved popular with the British, including the author Ian Fleming (1908–1964). He enjoyed writing in the hotel's Caid's Bar, which is named after General *(Caid)* Sir Harry Maclean (1848–1920), Scottish military advisor to several Moroccan sultans.

Other historic hotels in Tangier include the Grand Hôtel Villa de France, the Villa Josephine, the Fairmont Tazi Palace, and the Villa Muniria (see nos. 23, 30, 40, 35). Another is the 1940s-era Villa Mabrouka at 1 Sidi Bouknadel (Marshan), a boutique hotel hideaway with magical walled gardens that once belonged to fashion designer Yves Saint Laurent (1936–2008) and his partner Pierre Bergé (1930–2017). Sadly, the grand seafront Hotel Cecil, where Sultan Mohammed V (1909–1961) stayed in 1947, whilst making his plea for Moroccan independence, has been demolished (see no. 19).

Other locations nearby: 8, 10, 11, 12

10 Bath Houses and Bread Ovens

Medina (Old City), the Dar Baroud traditional hammam at 77 Rue Dar Baroud

In medinas across Morocco the same five communal public spaces have long existed: mosque *(jami)*, school *(madrassa)*, drinking fountain *(saqiyah)*, bath house *(hammam)*, and communal bread oven *(ferrane)*. Whilst the mosque and school remain central to Moroccan society, the fountain is today largely ornamental, and the bath house and oven are gradually being sidelined in favour of home appliances. Fortunately for visitors in search of traditional Tangier, a few examples of these once-commonplace features can still be found.

A traditional hammam on Rue dar Baroud

The *hammam* is strongly associated with the Muslim countries of the Maghreb. Originally part of the Muslim purification ritual, it later satisfied a more prosaic demand for weekly cleansing and socialising, especially in the days before private homes had piped water. Popular in Ottoman-era Turkey and long before that in ancient Rome, the *hammam* originally consisted of a series of hot and cold rooms – *Tepidarium* (warm room), *Caldarium* (hot room), and *Frigidarium* (cold room) – used to relax the muscles and joints, stimulate the blood, and exfoliate the skin.

Two of the oldest Moroccan *hammams* can be found not far from Tangier. The Hammam Sidi el-Mandri in Tétouan and the Hammam Ben Azouz in Chefchaouen were both established during the 15th century. Simple, single-room establishments, they are far removed from the glitz of modern-day hotel *hammams*, with their gleaming marble, fluffy robes, and fragrant candles. Tangier also retains a couple of old-school neighbourhood *hammams* albeit not nearly so old. One can be found tucked away on Rue Dar Baroud in the north-east corner of the Medina. Its horseshoe-shaped door sits alongside a sturdy stone archway claimed to be Roman although more likely Portuguese.

Whatever their age, the *hammams* of Tangier offer a time-honoured experience that remains essentially the same. Firstly, in preparation, one should purchase from a market or chemist a quantity of glutinous black olive soap *(savon beldi)* and an exfoliation glove *(kessa)* (try Maison Boukhari at 12 Rue Seqaya Jdida). Once inside the *hammam*, the sexes are segrated (or else they attend at different times), and strip down to their underwear (bring a spare pair for afterwards). Customers then enter a large tiled room that is hot and steamy, where they sit for a while as their skin softens. The attendants then throw buckets of water over them and apply the black soap, and exfoliate the skin rigorously using the glove. This is followed by a deep massage of the muscles with oil and the hair is washed followed by a final dowsing with water.

Like the *hammam*, the communal bread oven is also an increasingly rare sight. It was once common to see youngsters in the street carrying trays of their mothers' raw dough to the local baker, whose oven often heated the water for the neighbourhood *hammam*. A working example of a communal bread oven can be found at the corner of Rue Oudrass and Rue Cheikh Mohamed Ben Seddik (see page 2). Fired with wood, the brick-lined oven is long, so that plenty of dough can be slid far back into it on a wooden paddle. The resulting circular flatbreads are known as *msemmen*. Once the oven cools, other dishes such as casseroles and cookies can be slow cooked.

Of the modern *hammams* in Tangier, the two most atmospheric are in the Kasbah. They are La Tangerina at Rue Riad Sultan 19, with its *zellij* wall tiles and impressive dome, and L'Abyssin de Tanger at 22 Rue Tenaker, with its tranquil pool.

Other locations nearby: 9, 11, 12

11 The Brotherhoods of Dar Baroud

Medina (Old City), a selection of holy shrines in and around the neighbourhood of Dar Baroud

There is nothing visible in the Medina of Tangier that predates the late-15th century presence of the Portuguese. Despite this, there are areas where the street scene appears timeless. A good example is the Dar Baroud neighbourhood in the Medina's north-east corner. Here can be found a public bath *(hammam)*, communal bread oven *(ferrane)*, and several holy shrines *(zawiya)* that, together with the mosque *(jami)*, religious school *(madrassa)*, and public fountain *(saqiyah)*, are features once common to every neighbourhood in every medina across Morocco (see no. 10).

What concern us here are the holy shrines. The Arabic word *zawiya* meaning 'corner' or 'nook' was originally used to describe the tiny cells of Christian monks. Later the meaning was extended to describe Sufi Islamic shrines, prayer rooms, and small mosques. Typically, a *zawiya* is concealed behind a green, horseshoe-shaped doorway, which is usually kept locked. Some have crenellations and a dome above, whilst inside is usually a rectangular room with niches for books and offerings. Generally speaking a *zawiya* is distinct from a *marabout*, which looks

The minaret of the Zawiya Sidi Ali Ben Daud

similar but is the tomb of a holy man (see no. 14).

Tangier's greatest concentration of *zawiyas* is in Dar Baroud. Two are located on Place Ben Daoud, formerly called Place de l'Arsenal because of its proximity to the Borj dar el-Baroud bastion (see no. 12). On the south side of this square stands the Zawiya and Mosque Sidi Ali Ben Daud, with its squat minaret overlooking a tiled public fountain. It is dedicated to a revered holy man from the Rif Mountains, who died in Tangier around 1885. On the west side is the Zawiya Harraqia dedicated to a lawyer named Chauni al-Harrak. A third *zawiya* can be found a little farther south at the junction of Rue Dar Baroud with Rue Cheikh Mohamed Ben Seddik. Called the Zawiya Kettania, it was built in 1904 by the Kettania Brotherhood, after its leader returned from a visit to Mecca. Founded in Fez in the late-19th century, the Brotherhood's influence spread quickly to Tangier, where its members initially met in the Marabout of Sidi Ben Raissoul. Not long afterwards they moved to their present location.

Two more *zawiyas* lie a couple of streets west. They are the Zawiya Kadiria on Rue Wargha and the Zawiya Sheikh Mohammed Ben Seddik on Rue Zaouiah Kadiria. The latter was built by the Darkaua Brotherhood, whose members sport henna-dyed beards.

Sufi brotherhoods first appeared in Morocco during the 16th century, each led by a charismatic *sheikh* (noble holy man) or *sharif* (direct descendant of the Prophet). They carried out cultural and religious work, and gained great favour among local communities. Even the Sultans came to them for advice, and were wary of those that became too popular. During the late-19th century, the French and Spanish authorities curried favour with the brotherhoods to quell local opposition. Little wonder that when the leader of a Brotherhood died, he was given his own shrine, which then became a focus for pilgrims.

Elsewhere in the Medina are the Zawiya Hamadcha on Rue Almansour, the Zawiya Tinjani on Rue Ben Abdessadak (Tangier's oldest brotherhood founded in pre-Islamic times), and the 18th century Zawiya and Mosque of the Nasiriyya Brotherhood on Rue Naciria. Especially attractive is the Zawiya of the Aissawa Brotherhood on Place Aissawa. Their penchant for handling snakes is colourfully depicted by the Spanish Orientalist Josep Tapiró (1836–1913) in his painting *Feast of the Aissawa* (1885).

Other locations nearby: 9, 10, 12

12 The Walls of the Medina

Medina (Old City), the Borj Dar el-Baroud Interpretation Centre of the Fortifications of Tangier at the junction of Avenue Mohammed VI and Route de la Plage Merkala (La Corniche)

Tangier's Medina is a labyrinth of narrow winding alleys and cul-de-sacs packed with shops, homes, workplaces, and shrines. The word *medina* from the Arabic for 'city' describes an old North African walled town around which a modern city has developed. Such is the case with Tangier. That said, Tangier's Medina is no static museum, indeed its inhabitants and their properties are always evolving. What has not changed significantly is the wall protecting them.

The earliest wall was built 2,000 years ago by the Romans. Although nothing visible remains, its footings were reused by those that followed, notably the Vandals, Byzantines, and Umayyad Arabs. The wall seen today dates largely from the Portuguese occupation of Tangier (1471–1661), when it was rebuilt and strengthened to reach its present length of just over 1.1 miles. Since 1684, the wall has been maintained by the Alawi Sultanate.

To discover more about the wall, visit the Borj Dar el-Baroud Interpretation Centre of the Fortifications of Tangier. Located in the

The Borj Dar el-Baroud Interpretation Centre of the Fortifications of Tangier

north-east corner of the Medina, the Borj Dar el-Baroud is the sturdiest of seven bastions *(borj)* punctuating the wall. Its name means 'The Tower of the House of Dynamite', a reference to ammunition stores once located nearby. Today, the bastion's three stepped cannon batteries provide the perfect backdrop for a collection of maps, photographs, weapons, and uniforms illustrating the Medina's fortifications. Several 20-ton Armstrong Cannons installed in 1880 are still in place (see back cover).

From the scale models on display it is immediately apparent that the strongest bastions were built between the north-west and south-east corners, facing the sea whence an enemy attack was most likely. This explains the Borj en-Nâam, a bastion-cum-18th-century barracks protecting the north-west corner. It has recently been repurposed as the Exhibition Space in Memory of Ibn Battouta, the great Tangier-born medieval traveller (see no. 14). The Bab el-Bhar (Sea Gate), the only gate in the north wall, stands nearby although it was only inserted during the 1920s to provide access from the Kasbah to the sea cliffs. Offering wonderful views, it is said to be haunted by a female spirit *(djinn)* called Aisha Kandisha.

The eastern wall of the Medina was originally lapped by the sea. Today, however, it is high and dry, overlooking a broad reclaimed quayside along which runs Avenue Mohammed VI. There are several bastions and gates here, which are best appreciated from outside the Medina. From north to south they are: the Borj al-Salam over which sits the Hotel Continental; the Borj el-Hajoui flanked by the Bab el-Hira and Bab el-Marsa gates, which connect the Medina with the Old Port; the Bab dar Dbagh named for the tanneries that functioned here until the 1930s; and Bab Mérican, which gives access to the Old American Legation (see no. 4). At the southern tip of the Medina stands the Irish Tower added during the British occupation of Tangier (1661–1684).

The landward walls on the west side of the Medina were more lightly fortified. Accordingly, there are just two bastions here. The Borj Kathrine rises above the Central Market (Marché Central), as well as the main gates into the Medina, namely the 18th-century Bab al-Fahs ('checking gate' since incoming goods coming from caravanserais in the Grand Socco would be monitored here) and the Bab Fondaq Zraa, which opens onto Rue Siaghine, the Medina's main west–east thoroughfare. Farther north there are three gates: the Bab Rahbat Zraa, Bab Gzenaya, and Bab el-Kasbah. The latter, in the north-west corner of the Medina, is protected by the Borj Ben Amar, which completes this tour of the walls.

Other locations nearby: 9, 10, 11

13 Perfume, Carpets, and Candles

Medina (Old City), a tour of artisan and antique shops beginning at the Madini perfume shop at 14 Rue Sebou

The walled Medina is the oldest and for many visitors the most atmospheric area of Tangier. A part of its appeal is undoubtedly the idiosyncratic shops it contains. They reflect the city's artisanal traditions, such as perfume, carpets, candles, and ceramics, and in the Medina it is possible to see some of these products being made.

First stop is the Madini perfume shop at 14 Rue Sebou. This *Parfumerie Orientale* was established in 1919 by immigrants from Saudi Arabia. They supplied perfume to the well-to-do families and celebrities in the city at the time. Still in the hands of the Madini family, the current owners are justifiably proud of the bespoke perfumes they concoct using time-honoured Saudi traditions. Customers trial scents from the many glass bottles lining the walls: patchouli, amber, musk oil, oud resin, and rose essence among many others. Those they like are then decanted into a bottle of their own at the antique wooden counter. Although Madini now has a second larger outlet on Boulevard Pasteur (Ville Nouvelle), it is these original premises that offer the more authentic experience.

Perfumer Younes Hariri Madini at Madini on Rue Sebou

Next stop is Bleu de Fes at 65 Rue Almohades, one of many shops in the Medina selling carpets. The carpet business is a competitive one, so buyers should keep their wits about them, be sure what they are buying, and always haggle. In terms of customer service, Bleu de Fes is one of the best, offering a fine selection of handwoven Berber rugs.

Typically, they are flat-woven rather than pile rugs, with zig-zag, diamond, and lozenge patterns, as well as bold, simple geometric designs. Flat-weave rugs are known as *kilims* or *hanbels*, rugs which combine flat-weave with pile are called *zanafi* or *glaoua*, and rugs with black-and-white bands incorporating tapestry are *shedwi*. Another good carpet shop is Jabal Rif de Tanja at 12 Rue Hadj Mohamed Torres.

On the same street as Bleu de Fes, at number 66, is Boutique Majid. Tangier's most famous antique shop, it was opened in 1970 by Majid Rais el Fenni. The place is bursting with old textiles, leatherwork, ceramics, wooden doors and shutters, glassware, jewelry, and other decorative items. More than just a shop, it is a museum of Moroccan traditional crafts.

Different again is Rumi towards the top of Rue Amrah. Only handmade fragrant candles are sold here, each provided in a so-called *Beldi* glass. With their characteristic swollen midriff, these distinctive vessels were pioneered in the 1940s for use with mint tea. An unusual sight on Rue Amrah is that of tailors *(khiyat)* in their tiny workshops, their threads stretching far out into the street. There is also a woodworker here, too, who handcrafts frames inlaid with mother-of-pearl shell (see page 2).

Morocco's ceramic tradition stretches back to 10th century Fez, when intricate hand-made mosaics known as *zellij* were used to decorate palace walls. Less common in Tangier, a *zellij* workshop can nevertheless be found a short way up Avenue Ibn Al Abar, just west of the Medina.

Opposite the El Minzah Hotel at 72 Rue de la Liberté (Ville Nouvelle) is Galerie Tindouf. Like Boutique Masjid it is an antique hunter's paradise offering everything from brass lanterns and painted Berber coffers to copper cauldrons and salvaged ceramics. During the 1960s the Rolling Stones came here in search of old fabrics to have made into cushions! Just as alluring is Artingis at 11 Rue Khalid Ibn Oualid, with its carefully-curated selection of old books, photographs, and other collectibles documenting old Morocco.

Other locations nearby: 2, 5, 6, 14, 15

14 The Tomb of Ibn Battouta

Medina (Old City), the tomb of Ibn Battouta at the end of Rue Ibn Battouta, off Rue Faqui Abbadi (note: the tomb is kept locked although a key is held locally for Muslim pilgrims)

Observant visitors to Tangier will notice a recurring name: Ibn Battouta (sometimes Battuta). There is the Ibn Battouta shopping mall, sports stadium, airport, ferry, and a reservoir in Zinat that provides Tangier with its drinking water. In the Medina there is also a large wall mural of Ibn Battouta accompanied by a map of the world (see back cover). To discover why this man is omnipresent one should first visit the Exhibition Space in Memory of Ibn Battouta housed inside the Borj en-Nâam, a converted 18th-century fortification in the north-west corner of the Kasbah (see no. 12).

The well-hidden tomb of traveller Ibn Battouta

Born in Tangier during the time of the Marinid Dynasty (1244–1465), Ibn Battouta (1304–1368/1369 or 1377) was the greatest traveller of the medieval Muslim world. His name means literally 'son of the duckling' (*ibn* being 'son of' in the Classical Arabic of the *Qur'an*). Precious little is known about his early years other than that his father was a legal scholar of Berber descent. What is documented, however, is that between 1325 and 1354 he made a journey covering some 73,000 miles, which took in the equivalent of forty-four modern nations. He first travelled across North Africa and the Middle East to Mecca, then on into Russia, Central Asia, and China, before returning via Sri Lanka, the Maldives, and East Africa to Morocco. After a pause he then continued across the Sahara to West Africa and finally headed home. As such, he eclipsed by a long way the near-contemporary journeys of Marco Polo (1254–1324) and Zheng He (1371–1433).

Once back in Tangier, he set about dictating a monumental account of his journeys from memory. This was published in 1355 as *Travels in Asia and Africa 1325–1354: A Gift to Those Who Contemplate the Wonders of Cities and the Marvels of Travelling*. A mixture of detailed personal observation, anecdotal hearsay, history, and poetry, it is today known more simply as *El Riḥlah* (The Travels).

Ibn Battouta is believed to have died of bubonic plague in 1368/69 or perhaps later in 1377. Mystery surrounds his place of burial, with some commentators suggesting that he rests at the old Roman port of Anfa, now lost beneath the streets of Casablanca. Since Tangier was his home town, however, it seems more likely that he was buried there and indeed his purported tomb *(marabout)* can be found in the Medina. There are two ways to reach the tomb, which is in the Yenan Kaptan neighbourhood, in the north-western reaches of the Medina. From the Petit Socco, walk north along Rue Almohades, then turn left on to Rue Ben Abdessadak, right on to Rue Faqui Abbadi, and then continue northwards to join Rue Ibn Battouta, where the tomb will be found perched on a sharp corner at the end of the street. Alternatively enter the Medina through the Bab Gzenaya, off Rue d'Italie, then turn immediately left onto Rue Gzenaya to join Rue Faqui Abbadi.

The tomb of Ibn Battouta is not the only Islamic tomb *(marabout)* in the Medina. Others can be found in the Dar Baroud and Beni Idder neighbourhoods, as well as in the Kasbah (see nos. 4, 15, 17). More usually they contain local Muslim saints *(wali)*, whose descendants maintain the tomb as a site of pilgrimage. In this respect, a *marabout* resembles a *zawiya*, which is a Sufi shrine established by one of Tangier's long-standing brotherhoods. (see no. 11). Both often but not always take the form of a domed chamber *(qubba)*.

Other locations nearby: 13, 15, 16, 17

15 Partying with Barbara Hutton

Medina (Old City), the Sidi Hosni Palace on Rue Sidi Hassani (note: the palace is not open to the public but can be viewed from the street and neighbouring rooftops)

At the top of the Medina, opposite Café Baba on Rue Sidi Hassani, there stands a tall white house clad in bougainvillea. Known as the Sidi Hosni Palace, it once belonged to the wealthy American heiress Barbara Hutton (1912–1979). Nicknamed the "Poor Little Rich Girl" by the media due to her troubled private life, her time in Tangier added to the city's 20th century reputation as a bolthole and playground for lotus-eating expatriates.

Born in New York City, Hutton was heiress to one-third of the estate of her grandfather, the department store tycoon Frank Winfield Woolworth (1852–1919). This made her one of the wealthiest women in the world. Despite this she had an unhappy childhood blighted by the early loss of her mother and the neglect of her philandering father (although he did give her a 240-foot yacht for her 18th birthday followed by a cheque for a million dollars). Such unpredictable and unhealthy behaviour set the stage for a life of failed relationships during which she was married and divorced

The roof terrace at the Sidi Hosni Palace

seven times. Despite being envied for her privileged lifestyle, Hutton remained deeply insecure, taking refuge in lavish spending, parties, and affairs.

None of Hutton's marriages lasted more than four years. In 1946, following her divorce from film star Cary Grant (1904–1986), she escaped to Tangier, where she purchased the Sidi Hosni Palace to console herself. No ordinary home, it consisted of seven separate properties merged into one by the previous owner, whose six Spanish servants were included in the sale. The palace included rooms on various levels, as well as several shaded patios, and whitewashed, crenellated roof terraces.

It was on the roof, with its far-reaching views across the Medina to the ocean, that Hutton hosted extravagant parties. Helped in their planning by flamboyant British socialite David Herbert (1908–1995), a typical guest list might include American ambassadors, cabarettists, wartime spies, hairdressers, and all manner of libertines. Hutton gave Herbert a Cadillac for his birthday, which, like Hutton's Rolls Royce, necessitated the Medina's alleys be widened to accommodate it!

It was in Tangier that Hutton met and married her seventh and final husband, the Laotian Prince Pierre Raymond Doan Vinh na Champassak. This marriage, too, foundered and they divorced two years later. It was now clear to Hutton that she would never escape her demons, a realisation made worse in 1972 when her only child perished in a plane crash. A life of extravagance and generosity combined with exploitation by those entrusted to manage her estate rendered Hutton almost bankrupt by the time of her death in 1979. It is said that she wanted to be buried in Tangier, one of the few places she found a measure of happiness, but instead she spent her final years in Los Angeles. She was laid to rest in the Woolworth family mausoleum at Woodlawn Cemetery in New York.

The name of the Sidi Hosni Palace comes from the white-domed tomb-cum-shrine *(marabout)* of Sidi Hosni, a local holy man and a relative of the Sharif of Ouezzane. The tomb was installed around 1890 in Sidi Hosni's home, which stood alongside the palace. Another *marabout* belonging this time to Sidi Ben Raissoul stands nearby at the junction of Rue Amrah and Rue Sidi Jalil. Unusually its Mecca-facing apse *(mihrab)* projects outwards at first floor level on account of the sloping terrain.

Other locations nearby: 13, 14, 16, 17

16 Samuel Pepys' Fig Tree

Kasbah (Old City), Dar Zero on Place de la Kasbah (note: the property is private but can be viewed from outside as well as from the roof terrace of the nearby Macondo restaurant)

Not all Western visitors to Tangier have been enamoured of the place. St Francis of Assisi (c. 1181–1226) decried its "madness and delusions" and Gavin Maxwell (1914–1969), author of *A Ring of Bright Water*, complained that "Life here is hell". The diarist Samuel Pepys (1633–1703) thought God should destroy Tangier, which he branded the "excresence of the earth". Pepys' unhappy time, however, represents an important chapter in the city's story.

In 1662, Tangier passed from the Portuguese to the English as part of Catherine of Braganza's dowry to her husband, King Charles II (1630–1685). To maximise the financial return from his new acquisition, the king declared Tangier open to free trade and constructed a seawall to shelter visiting merchant vessels. The walled Medina was protected by a garrison of 2,000 troops and surrounded by a series of defensive redoubts.

Despite such precautions, the English colony faced the continual threat of attack by local tribal forces not to mention the high cost of maintaining a garrison so far from home. The greatest threat came from the Berber warlord Khadir Ghailan (1599–1672). Already in 1656, he had surrounded the Medina in a failed attempt to expel the Portuguese and create a north Moroccan emirate.

Dar Zero on Place de la Kasbah

Whereas the Portuguese ruled Tangier from 1471 until 1661, the English lasted barely two decades. Twice, in 1662 and 1664, Ghailan routed Anglo-Irish troops at Merkala Beach (see no. 39). Ghailan's ambitions, however, were eventually foiled by the rise of the Alawi Sultanate. In 1673, he was defeated and killed by the army of Sultan Ismail Ibn Sharif (1645–1727). Now it was the sultan's turn to harry the English, which he did successfully in 1675 and again in 1680. The result was a four-year truce at the end of which the British abandoned Tangier.

The man chosen to orchestrate the evacuation was Samuel Pepys. His talent for administration rather than seafaring saw him become Chief Secretary to the Admiralty. As the most senior civil servant in the Navy, he assisted the Governor of Tangier with the evacuation and destruction of Tangier's British infrastructure. Six months later, the Muslim resettlement began.

During his stay, Pepys spent time at the Portuguese-built Governor's House, renamed York Castle during the 1660s by the British. Located on the cobble-stoned square outside the Kasbah palace, it was near here beneath a fig tree that Pepys wrote part of his famous ten-year-long diary. The gnarled tree still stands in the courtyard of an adjacent property, known as Dar Zero because of its unusual house number.

As well as its connection with Pepys, Dar Zero has seen a string of noteworthy occupants. During the first half of the 20th century, it was home to British author Richard Hughes (1900–1976) of *A High Wind in Jamaica* (1929) fame. He was followed by eccentric English watercolourist Jim Wyllie, who for a time rented it out to photographer and costumier Cecil Beaton (1904–1980). In 1961, American interior designer Charles Sevigny (1918–2019) and his companion Knoll Furniture director Yves Vidal (1923–2001) acquired Dar Zero as a guesthouse for York Castle, which they had occupied since the 1950s. When in 1996 York Castle was rendered uninhabitable following a landslip (it is largely ruined today), the pair relocated to Dar Zero. After years of visiting, fellow designers, Jamie Creel (b. 1966) and Marco Scarani (b. 1972) purchased the house with the proviso that Sevigny could stay on for his lifetime. Creel and Scarani still spend time there today. Although Dar Zero is not open to the public, Pepys' fig tree still rises above the building's whitewashed outer walls.

Other locations nearby: 14, 15, 17

17 Up at the Kasbah

Kasbah (Old City), a tour of the Kasbah including the Museum of Mediterranean Cultures (Musée des Cultures Méditerranéennes) on Place de la Kasbah

At the highest point of the Medina, overlooking the Strait of Gibraltar, is the Kasbah. Protected by its own set of fortifications, this citadel was the political and military centre of the Old City. Shadowy remains attest to the strategic importance of the site since at least Roman times (see no. 33). During the 10th century, the Umayyad Emir of Córdoba, Abd al-Rahman III (890–961), installed a maritime surveillance post here, which was followed in the 12th century by an Almohad-era palace. The Portuguese then built a governor's residence when they took Tangier in 1471 (see no. 12). When the English arrived two centuries later, they renamed the residence York Castle and built a palace, which they demolished when they departed in 1684.

In the 1730s, under the orders of Alawi Sultan Ismail Ibn Sharif (1645–1727), Pasha Ahmed Ben Ali al-Rifi (1691–1740), Governor of Tangier, built the present Governor's Palace (Dar al-Makhzen) over the ruins of its English predecessor. Part of the Muslim resettlement and reconstruction of the city, this new palace was surrounded by administrative buildings, as well as a mosque, barracks, stables, prison, and military residential quarters. It formed the central element of a self-contained

Elaborate decoration inside the Governor's Palace

governmental quarter suitable for use by visiting sultans. The palace was restored in 1889, when Sultan Hassan I (1836–1894) made Tangier the country's diplomatic capital. Since 1922, when the exiled Sultan Abd al-Hafid (1875–1937) deemed the palace too small for his retinue of 168 wives, concubines, and servants, it has been a public museum.

The Kasbah is book-ended by two public squares: Place du Tabor, which opens onto the Marshan via the Bab el-Kasbah, and Place de la Kasbah, which is accessed from the Medina by either the Bab el-Assa (Gate of the Stick), where wrongdoers were once flogged, or the Bab Haha. The Bab el-Assa, where this tour begins, is the most photogenic of the Kasbah gates and was painted to great effect by French artist Georges Bretegnier (1860–1892). Just inside is a bench decorated with colourful *zellij* tiles. From here turn left across the square imagining its original use as a ceremonial parade ground. The entrance to the palace is flanked by a triple-arched courthouse, where government affairs were carried out (today the eclectic Galerie Laure Welfling design store), and a treasury *(bayt al-mal)* reached by a flight of stairs.

The Andalusian Garden at the Governor's Palace

Hispano-Moorish in style, the palace is centred on a large central courtyard decorated with *zellij* tilework and a marble fountain. The ornate column capitals were imported from Italy. Ranged around the courtyard are seven reception rooms lavishly decorated with carved stucco, more *zellij*, and two intricately carved cedarwood domes known as *muqarnas*. These rooms are home to the Museum of Mediterranean Cultures (Musée des Cultures Méditerranéennes), which contains artefacts illustrating the history of Tangier from prehistoric times up to the 20th century. As well as Stone Age flint tools, Roman ships' anchors, handwritten manuscripts, and suits of armour, there is a magnificent seafaring mosaic from the Roman city of Volubilis.

To the rear of the palace is a tranquil Andalusian-style garden, fragrant with citrus and fig trees, and home to cooing doves and lumbering tortoises. The garden can also be seen from the café terrace of the Théâtre Riad Sultan, an intimate cultural space on Rue Riad Sultan.

Two other elements make up the palace complex. The 18th century Kasbah Mosque (Jami' al-Qasba) stands on Rue Ibn Abbou, which extends beyond the palace entrance. It features a horseshoe-shaped main entrance decorated with *zellij* and a minaret that is octagonal rather than square. Its sides are decorated with blind arches filled with green, yellow, and blue tiles, above which are panels of *sebka* geometric motifs. Note the nearby École Fatima al Fihria, a *madrassa* affiliated to the University of Qarawiyyin, which was founded in 859 in Fez and is, according to UNESCO, the oldest, continually operating educational institution in the world.

The Kasbah's 17th century prison, which faces onto the Place de la Kasbah, remained in use until the early 1970s. With its barred windows still in place, it now serves as a contemporary art space celebrating northern Morocco's homegrown modernist art movement that blossomed during the 20th century. On display are works by the likes of Mohamed Ataallah (1939–2014) and Saâd Ben Cheffaj (b. 1939).

Behind the palace is the Kasbah's residential neighbourhood, where the streets are narrow like those in the Medina but less frenetic. There are several traditional Moroccan courtyard houses *(riads)* here that serve as charming boutique hotels. Highly recommended is the 300-year-old Dar Sultan on Rue Ahmed Ben Ajiba, with its seven individually-decorated bedrooms. Also in common with the Medina are the tombs of holy men *(marabouts)* (see no. 11). A fine example on the same street is the *marabout* Sidi Ahmed Bouqouja housing the tomb of a respected Qur'anic scholar. It is colourfully depicted in the painting *Le Marabout* by Henri Matisse (1869–1954).

Outside the Bab el-Kasbah are three shops that champion the best of new generation Moroccan crafts and design: Las Chicas at 52 Rue Kacem Guennoune sells quirky designer clothes, tableware, mirrors, and light fittings; Zackyshop at 46E promotes modern ceramics from southern Morocco; and the Kasbah Collective at 30 offers *babushka* slippers, funky ceramics, and handwoven throws.

Other locations nearby: 14, 15, 16

18 Around the Grand Socco

Ville Nouvelle (New City), a walk around the Grand Socco including the Sidi Bou Abid Mosque (Jami' Sidi Bou Abid) (note: this is a working mosque and closed to non-Muslims)

As the walled Medina has its Petit Socco, so the Ville Nouvelle beyond has its Grand Socco. Its alternative name, Souk al-Barra ('Outside Souk'), reflects this extramural location. Both once busy marketplaces, they are connected by Rue Semarine and Rue Siaghine, the latter being the Medina's main west–east axis dating back to Roman times (see nos. 6, 33). The word *socco* is the Moroccan rendering of the Spanish *zoco*, itself a corruption of the Arabic *souk* meaning market.

Unlike the Petit Socco, the Grand Socco is a relatively modern creation. Once described as the 'Gateway to Morocco', it only became an open-air market and traffic intersection during Tangier's early-20th century colonial period, when the Ville Nouvelle was laid out in European style. Before that the area was little more than a sloping, oval space, where visiting merchants offloaded their wares at caravanserais *(foundouks)*, Jebala women from the western Rif Mountains peddled their wares, and pilgrims paid homage at the

An old postcard showing the Grand Socco and the Bab al-Fahs (right)

tombs *(marabouts)* of holy men. Farmers brought their livestock here and charcoal burners were active on the slope above. Annual regional festivals *(moussems)* as well as boisterous equestrian *fantasias* attracted peddlers, water carriers, snake charmers, and storytellers. It must have been quite a sight.

As the Ville Nouvelle grew and became busier, so market activities were relocated to today's permanent Central Market (Marché Central) on the eastern edge of the Grand Socco. Today, the old marketplace functions as a large traffic island but one that has been made pedestrian friendly by the addition of benches, palm trees, lawns, and a fountain (see back cover). For an overview, walk to its highest point to what is known locally as La Terrasse, where older locals might be seen playing the Spanish board game *parchís*.

Despite the changes on the Grand Socco and an inevitable loss of character, there are still some interesting sights. Much of the west side of the square is taken up by the Sidi Bou Abid Mosque (Jami' Sidi Bou Abid). Completed in 1917 and incorporating the pre-existing *marabout* of the patron saint for whom the mosque is named, it was the first mosque built outside the walls of the Medina. The polychrome tilework on the minaret hangs like a giant Atlas Mountain carpet above the square.

As with the Petit Socco, there is a deliberate juxtaposition of mosque and market, a reminder of the involvement of Islam in everyday life. Since its relocation, the Central Market (Marché Central) has filled the east side of the square (see no. 18). Access from the Grand Socco is by means of the horseshoe-shaped Bab al-Fahs gate. Unlike its temporary predecessor, today's market is a permanent, covered, seven-days-a-week affair. Needless to say, it is a feast for the visitor's senses.

On the south side of the Grand Socco stands the Cinéma Rif, on a site formerly occupied by the 19th century Hotel Cavilla. Opened in 1938, the cinema was refurbished in 2007 and is today home to the Cinémathèque de Tanger (see no. 20).

Finally, on the north side of the square, is the Mendoubia Palace (Dar Mandubiya). Occupied by the sultan's representative during the time of the Tangier International Zone (1925–1956), it was in the gardens here on 9th April 1947 that Mohammed V (1909–1961) gave a speech in support of Moroccan independence (see no. 19). This explains the Grand Socco's official name: Place 9 Avril 1947.

Other locations nearby: 1, 2, 19, 20, 21

19 9th April 1947

Ville Nouvelle (New City), the Mendoubia Palace on the Grand Socco

On 9th April 1947, Sultan Mohammed V (1909–1961) made a speech in favour of Moroccan independence. At the time, Morocco was divided between French and Spanish Protectorates, with Tangier designated an International Zone (1925–1956). The speech was delivered in the Mendoubia Gardens, just off the Grand Socco, and reinforced a day later by a second speech given at the Grand Mosque in the Medina. Remarkably it was the first visit to Tangier by a Moroccan sultan since that of Hassan I (1836–1894) in 1889.

The background to the so-called Tangier Speech *(Discours de Tanger)* was years of European involvement in Moroccan affairs. As early as the 1840s, many European countries had established consulates in Tangier to facilitate commerce with North Africa. In 1872, the newly-established German Empire followed suit by establishing a consulate just outside the main entrance to the Medina. Ironically it was here in 1905 that Kaiser Wilhelm II (1859–1941) spoke out against growing French influence in Morocco. This led to the Algeciras Conference (1906) at which French involvement was affirmed.

In 1914, the German consul was expelled and his consulate expropriated. In 1920, the consulate was repurposed as the ceremonial premises of the *Naib*, the sultan's personal representative through whom his government *(Makhzen)* liaised with foreign diplomats (see no. 5). With the establishment of the Tangier International Zone in 1925, the office of the *Naib* was replaced by that of the *Mendoub*, whose task it was to govern the affairs of the city's predominantly Muslim and Jewish community. The premises of the *Naib* thus became those of the *Mendoub* and were rebranded as the Mendoubia Palace (Dar Mandubiya) (this should not be confused with the Mendoub's Residence (Dar al-Mandub) located up on the Marshan (see no. 35)).

In June 1940, following the fall of France, Tangier came under Spanish military administration, and the mandate of the *Mendoub* was abolished. General Franco (1892–1975) allowed the installation of a Nazi German consul in the Mendoubia Palace, who remained until his expulsion in 1944. The *Mendoub* returned in late 1945 and with him Tangier regained its International Status.

While Morocco still was not a sovereign state, an encouraging meeting in 1943 with American President Franklin Roosevelt prompted the sultan to form the Istiqlal ('Independence') Party and to draft a

The former Mendoubia Palace on the Grand Socco

manifesto calling for a constitutional monarchy with democratic institutions. The French authorities were up in arms but the sultan persisted resulting in his now-famous visit to Tangier in 1947. The 1953 installation by the French of a puppet sultan, Mohammed Ben Aarafa (1886–1976), was short-lived and in 1955 Moroccan independence was reluctantly approved.

Following the French-Moroccan Declaration of Independence on 2nd March 1956, the Grand Socco was officially renamed Place du 9 Avril to commemorate the sultan's speech. Since the *Mendoub* was no longer required, the Mendoubia Palace was repurposed as the city's commercial court. It has since been joined by a museum (Espace de la Mémoire historique de la résistance et de la libération à Tanger) in which artefacts, photos, and archival documents tell the story of Morocco's long road to freedom. In the courtyard there is a memorial stone inscribed with the text of the sultan's speech. The colossal banyan fig tree (*Ficus benghalensis*) alongside it is said to be 800 years old.

In the adjacent Mendoubia Gardens are the remains of Christian and Muslim cemeteries established during the 19th century and abandoned in 1911. Nearby Rue Sidi Bouabid is lined with noisy welding shops and ovens where sheep's heads and cow's feet are singed for use in a slow-cooked Moroccan stew known as *hergma*.

Other locations nearby: 1, 2, 18, 20, 21

20 The Cinéma Rif

Ville Nouvelle (New City), the Cinéma Rif on the Grand Socco

Tangier is the Moroccan city that has most inspired Western filmmakers. Indeed the first film ever made in Morooco, the French-made silent film *Mecktoub* (1919), was shot in Tangier. Such was the city's rackety reputation during the time of the Tangier International Zone (1925–1956) that many films traded on the name alone despite being filmed elsewhere. Titles such as *Tangier* (1946), *Flight to Tangier* (1953), and *That Man from Tangier* (1957) all capitalised on the fact that Tangier as a free port, with no customs restrictions or money controls, attracted gold and with it smugglers, traffickers, crooks, and other screen-friendly characters. *Ticket to Tangier*, an episode from Orson Welles' 1951 radio prequel to the film *The Third Man* (1949), did the same. There were Nazis, spies, and fugitives too, providing the plot for the most famous film of the period, *Casablanca* (1942), which despite its name depicts Tangier.

Tangier's shadowy reputation has persisted with Western filmmakers. Two James Bond films have been filmed in the city – *The Living Daylights* (1987) and *Spectre* (2015) – as has an instalment in the Jason Bourne franchise (see no. 29). Bond's creator, English writer Ian Fleming (1908–1964), spent the Second World War working for Britain's Naval Intelligence Division. As part of Operation Goldeneye, he set up a Tangier office to undertake sabotage operations in the event that Germany occupied Gibraltar. Fleming returned to Tangier after the war and stayed at the El Minzah Hotel, where he researched his non-fiction book *The Diamond Smugglers* (1957).

The Western contribution to the city's cinematic history should not be overstated though. The involvement of Moroccan film directors since the first Moroccan film was made in the late-1950s is considerable and nowhere better illustrated than at the Cinéma Rif on the Grand Socco (Ville Nouvelle). Opened in 1938 by the Spanish as the Cinema Rex, this eyecatching Art Deco-style picture house was renamed after the declaration of Moroccan independence in 1956. Having lost its majority-Spanish audience, however, it fell on hard times and by the early 2000s was reduced to playing sub-titled Bollywood films. Threatened with demolition, its lot improved in 2003, when Yto Barrada (b. 1971), an internationally renowned French-Moroccan artist, arrived on the scene. With a team of dedicated colleagues she renovated and upgraded the place, reinventing it as the non-profit La Cinémathèque de Tanger, North Africa's first arthouse cinema.

The Cinéma Rif today plays a key role in the artistic rebirth of Tangier. With its retro charm preserved, it now boasts an extensive Moroccan film archive and a very popular café decorated with posters of vintage Tangier-related films. With a focus on both mainstream and alternative films, one might just as easily watch Bernardo Bertolucci's *The Sheltering Sky* (1990) and the vampire film *Only Lovers Left Alive* (2013) here as Moumen Smihi's *El Chergui* (1975) or Ahmed El Maanouni's *Trances* (1981). Also available to both locals and visitors are filmmaking workshops, art exhibitions, lectures, and other events; the Cinéma Rif has become a true cultural hub.

The Cinéma Rif overlooking the Grand Socco

Tangier's other historic cinemas include the Cine Alcazar on Rue d'Italie (Ville Nouvelle), which opened as a theatre in 1913 before being converted to a cinema in 1917, and three street corner cinemas from the 1950s, the Goya, Mauritania, and Roxy, which can all be found in the Ville Nouvelle. All the rest have long since closed, including the seafront Tivoli, which in 1913 became the city's first dedicated picture house. The Vox in the Petit Socco had a bar that may have inspired Rick's Café Américain in *Casablanca*. Others included the Americano, Capitol, Dawliz, Flandria, Lux, Mabrouk, Paris, Tarik, and Zarzuela.

Other locations nearby: 1, 2, 18, 19, 21, 25

21 A Corner of a Foreign Field

Ville Nouvelle (New City), St. Andrew's Church on Rue d'Angleterre (note: to look inside the church ask the on-site warden)

The Anglican Church of St. Andrew is a charming reminder of the British presence in Tangier. Set within a flower-filled, walled graveyard on Rue d'Angleterre, it is an oasis of peace despite its central location. Its intriguing Anglo-Islamic style bears witness to the city's reputation for harmonious interfaith relations.

The original church was a prefabricated tin construction shipped from London in 1884 and erected on land donated to Queen Victoria by Sultan Hassan I (1836–1894). This was replaced a decade later by the present building, which displays a fusion of architectural styles. From a distance it appears straight out of an English country landscape (note the horse mounting block outside the gate). When one gets closer, however, it is apparent that the church tower is more in keeping with a Hispano-Moorish minaret. The belfry vents are Islamic-style keyhole windows surrounded by interlocking blind arches, the stepped crenellations are Middle Eastern in style, and the walls are decorated with panels of polychrome tiles. The roof is clad in green tiles in keeping with Moroccan holy structures.

A Union Jack flutters atop St. Andrew's Church

The interior of the church features the same

architectural synthesis. The cruciform plan is that of an English parish church whereas the decoration is strikingly Islamic. Carried out by craftsmen from Fez, the ornately-stuccoed horseshoe arch separating the nave from the chancel is framed by the Lord's Prayer in *Kufic* calligraphy. The chancel, which contains the altar and gold Crucifix, features a carved cedarwood ceiling with a central *muqarna*, and an apse in the form of a mosque's Mecca-facing niche *(mihrab)*. Note the wall plaque commemorating the English governess Emily Keene (1849–1944), who introduced the smallpox vaccine to Morocco and married the powerful Sharif of Ouezzane, Sidi Abdeslam (1834–1892). Another plaque recalls Squadron Leader Thomas Kirby-Green (1918–1944), one of the prisoners of war shot by the Gestapo in March 1944 following the 'Great Escape'.

The graveyard contains a diverse collection of headstones. The on-site warden will gladly point out the following: *The Times* correspondent and explorer Walter Burton Harris (1866–1933) and the sultan's Scottish military advisor Caid Sir Harry Maclean (1848–1920), both famously kidnapped by the Riffian bandit Raisuli; the Late Romantic artist George Apperley (1884–1960), who came to Tangier for the light and exoticism; Edward Taylor, who in 1878 built the first steam mill in Tangier to produce carbonated drinks; the former Chief Justice of Bombay Sir Basil Scott (1859–1926); the Birmingham-born gangster and bar owner Paul Axel Lund (1915–1966); the flamboyant socialite and second son of the Earl of Pembroke, David Herbert (1908–1995); the interior designer Christopher Gibbs (1938–2018), who coined the phrase 'Swinging London'; and the mysterious Dean of Dean's Bar fame (see nos. 30, 42, 50). Military graves include a group of 13 RAF pilots and ground crew killed in a single raid on Tangier during the Second World War.

Tangier's 40,000-strong British community has dwindled considerably since Moroccan independence in 1956. St. Andrew's is now without a permanent chaplain and the Sunday congregation barely numbers twenty, half of which is usually Nigerian refugees hoping to reach Europe. Church funds are stretched and the cracks in the walls need repairing. If you visit, please give what you can.

The English governess Emily Keene is buried in the private Ouezzane family cemetery opposite their former home, Dar Dâmânah, on the Marshan. The family also had homes in the Medina, namely on Place Taqaddum and on the site of the Hotel Continental (see nos. 4, 9).

Other locations nearby: 1, 18, 19, 20, 25

22 Art in the New City

Ville Nouvelle (New City), some contemporary art collections including Galerie Delacroix at 86 Rue de la Liberté

When it comes to art and artists in Tangier, it is easy to get wrapped up in the story of the 19th century Orientalists and the Fauvist Matisse (1869–1954). They, of course, are only a part of the story, and one viewed inevitably through a European lens (see no. 23). After being influenced by these travelling artists, homegrown Moroccan art came of age during the 20th century. Having successfully broken the chains of Islamic art, it is today the dominant genre as witnessed by the very different canvasses hanging in the galleries and art shops of the Ville Nouvelle (New City) (see nos. 23, 50).

A work by Belgian-Moroccan artist Amina Rezki at the Galerie Delacroix

Highly recommended is the Galerie Delacroix at 86 Rue de la Liberté. An extension of the French Institute of Tangier, it promotes emerging and established Moroccan talent. Artists and sculptors such as Abdellah El-Haitout (b. 1971), Abdelghani Bouzian (b. 1978), and Najoua El Hitmi (b. 1978) have all benefited from having their work exhibited here in the handful of elegant, light-filled rooms. Within easy walking distance from here are Galerie Dar d'Art at 6 Rue Khalil Matrane, Gallery Kent at 19 Rue Jabha Wataniya, and Galeria Cervantes at 8 Avenue Belgique. All three stage temporary exhibitions that reflect and champion Tangier's present-day artistic soul.

An offbeat venue to enjoy contemporary Moroccan art is Galerie d'Art Contemporain Mohamed Drissi at 52 Rue d'Angleterre. It is housed in the former British Consulate, which was completed in 1892 to replace earlier premises opened in 1783 in the Medina (note the Moorish fountain pavilion in the public square opposite dedicated to the memory of Sir Reginald Lister (1865–1912), a former British ambassador to Morocco). After the consulate closed in the 1970s, its former ground floor reception rooms were converted into Morocco's first gallery of contemporary art. It was subsequently named in honour of artist Mohamed Drissi (1946–2003), who led renovation work in 2006. Seasonal exhibitions are the norm here and have featured abstract works by Farid Belkahia (1934–2014), Mohammed Kacimi (1942–2003), Abdelkebir Rabia (b. 1944), Mohammed Abdallah Hariri (b. 1949), Fouad Bellamine (b. 1950), and female artists Chaibia Tallal (1929–2004) and Fatima Hassan El Farouj (1945–2011). French artists have also been showcased here, including the modern Orientalists Louis Riou (1893–1958), Henri Pontoy (1888–1968), and Patrice Laurioz (b. 1959).

The Medina and Kasbah might not immediately be associated with modern art. That said, Galerie Conil has three locations here: 35 Rue des Almohades, 7 Rue du Palmier, and the junction of Rue Ahmed Ben Ajiba and Rue Ibn Abbou. All showcase contemporary and outsider art by local mixed-media artists, including paintings, bronzes, and *art brut*. A notable artist whose work has been featured here is Abdeljalil Boussaki (b. 1960).

Tangier has not shied away from street art. Easy to identify are the stick figures adorning numerous electricity fuse boxes in the Medina and Kasbah. They are the work of the artist Punksy (real name Samir Douass). Most impressive is the Leila Alaoui Mural, which covers the side of a six-storey tower block at the junction of Boulevard Mohammed V and Avenue Youssef Ibn Tachfine (Ville Nouvelle). The work of Moroccan street artist Mouad Aboulhana (b. 1989), it commemorates a talented young Moroccan-French photographer, Leila Alaoui (1982–2016), who was killed in a terrorist attack in Burkina Faso, where she was working for Amnesty International.

Other locations nearby: 20, 21, 23, 24

23 The View from Room 35

Ville Nouvelle (New City), the Matisse Room in the Grand Hôtel Villa de France at the junction of Rue d'Angleterre and Rue de Hollande

For the last two centuries, foreign artists have been visiting North Africa. Morocco in general has provided much visual inspiration with its luminous sunlight, earthy hues, distinctive architecture, and local colour. Tangier has proved especially popular because of its proximity to Europe.

One of the first to arrive was the French Romantic artist Eugène Delacroix (1798–1863). In 1832, he travelled to Morocco as part of a diplomatic mission following the French conquest of Algeria. Although he visited primarily to experience a non-European culture, he returned home with more than a hundred watercolours and drawings, which he worked up later in oils in his studio. One work entitled *The Convulsionists of Tangier* (1838) depicts the frenzied devotional activities of members of the Aissawa Sufi Brotherhood (see no. 11). It typifies the Orientalist style in vogue at the time through which exoticised local scenes were created as a visual accompaniment to European colonialism.

Other Orientalists who visited Tangier included the French artists Georges Bretegnier (1860–1892) and Jean-Joseph Benjamin-Constant (1845–1902). There was John Singer Sargent (1856–1925), too, who around the same time recorded Moroccan bedouins, goatherds, and fishermen, long before he found fame in America as a society portrait painter.

The foreign artist most associated with Tangier, however, is the *avant-garde* Fauvist Henri Matisse (1869–1954). He visited several months a year between 1911 and 1913 and was instantly captivated by the place, describing it as "a painter's paradise". Arriving in the midst of a storm, he took a room at the Grand Hôtel Villa de France, formerly home to the French Ambassador, which still stands at the junction of Rue d'Angleterre and Rue de Hollande (Ville Nouvelle). Almost immediately he painted a still life of a vase of irises on his dressing table.

Far from being an Orientalist, Matisse deployed animated brushwork, thin washes of pigment, and a palette of bright colours. Such choices were ideally suited to the scenes he encountered in Tangier, which resulted in some twenty oil paintings and many more sketches. His *La Porte de la Casbah* (The Kasbah Gate) could not be more different from the same scene rendered by the Orientalist Bretegnier two decades earlier. His *Vue sur la Baie de Tanger* (View of the Bay of Tangier) is similarly striking for its modernity, as is his best-known Tangier work *Paysage vu d'une Fenêtre* (Landscape viewed from a Window). Rendered mainly in various blues and with little attention to perspective, it depicts the view from Room 35 at the Grand Hôtel Villa de France, looking out over St. Andrew's Church, with the Medina beyond (the room can be rented and includes copies of works by Matisse on the wall). Although Matisse spent only a matter of months at a time in Tangier, the experience informed much of his subsequent work.

The view from the Grand Hôtel Villa de France by Henri Matisse

A very different foreigh artist in Tangier was Francis Bacon (1909–1992), who followed his partner Peter Lacy, a former RAF pilot, to the city in 1956. Their tempestuous relationship resulted in a series of dark and disturbing works painted later in London by Bacon, including *Pope* (1958) and *Landscape near Malabata* (1963).

It would be wrong not to mention here two self-taught Moroccan artists associated with Tangier. Mohammed Ben Ali R'bati (1861–1939) has been described as "the father of Moroccan painting" for his scenes of Tangier rendered in a fusion of traditional and European influences. Mohammed Hamri (1932–2000) is remembered for his bold, cheerful depictions of the Moroccan people.

Other locations nearby: 20, 21, 22, 24, 25

24 Fresh Fish and Pigeon Pie

Ville Nouvelle (New City), a culinary tour including Restaurant Populaire Le Saveur de Poisson at 2 Escalier Waller (note: booking is necessary to avoid disappointment)

The Moroccan kitchen is known for its distinctive and flavourful dishes. It is the result not only of the country's rich natural resources but also its interaction with other cultures and the desire by its Imperial courts to embellish their local cuisine accordingly.

Two thousand years ago the Berber (more correctly Amazigh) people, Morocco's earliest inhabitants, integrated couscous (semolina made from durum wheat flour), chickpeas, and beans into their diet. They also introduced the *tagine*, an earthenware cooking vessel with a conical lid used for slow cooking. During the 8th century AD, the Arabs imported pungent Asian spices such as cumin, cloves, pepper, ginger, and turmeric, as well as the Persian penchant for nuts and dried fruits. Around the same time, the proximity of Morocco to Moorish Spain encouraged an increased production of olives and olive oil. In 1492, when the Jews were evicted from Spain, they brought with them pickling techniques and, during the brief Ottoman presence, grilled skewers were added to the repertoire. In 1912, when most of Morocco became a French Protectorate, ice cream and patisseries were added. Even British roast beef made a

Food preparation at Restaurant Populaire Le Saveur de Poisson

brief appearance during the time of the Tangier International Zone (1925–1956), when it became a menu mainstay at the popular Giutta's Restaurant.

The epicurean traveller will encounter various signature Moroccan dishes. They include: *tagine* (baked chicken, lamb, or beef served with steamed couscous and vegetables); *bistilla* (chicken, pigeon, or quail pie containing nuts, cinnamon, orange blossom water, and a dusting of sugar); *sfiria* (lamb with honey); *rfissa* (chicken with lentils and day-old bread); and *mechoui* (whole spit-roasted sheep). Soups are plentiful, too, including *harira* (lentil and chickpea), *bissara* (fava bean and split green pea), *loubia* (bean), and *belboula* (barley). Several of these dishes will be found at the better visitor-friendly restaurants in and around the Medina, including the laid back Chez Hassan at 8 Rue de la Kasbah, the upmarket Hammadi around the corner with its traditional musicians, and the cosy, family-run Kebdani on Rue der Baroud.

There are two decidedly modest places in the Ville Nouvelle (New City) that come highly recommended. Restaurant Bachir at 51 Rue Zyriab is more a canteen than a restaurant but it offers excellent, freshly-cooked Moroccan food at a fair price and with friendly service. Ignore the plastic table-clothes and commotion, and instead enjoy piping hot bowls of soup, chicken *tagines* with olives, and sizzling kebabs. Equally authentic is the Restaurant Populaire Le Saveur de Poisson tucked away at 2 Escalier Waller. The set meals here (there is no menu) typically consist of warm bread and olives, fish soup, fried calamari, or anchovies, and platters of grilled monkfish, hake, or red mullet. The fish is very fresh since it comes direct from the nearby market (see no. 1). Dessert might be fruit and sweetened couscous *(seffa)* washed down with home-made prune juice. Before the restaurant opened there was a lock-up here owned by a hashish dealer called Achmed Hamifsah. During the late-1960s, he famously supplied Brian Jones and Keith Richards of the Rolling Stones (see no. 34). If a table is not available try Al Achab at 30 Avenue Prince Moulay Abdellah.

Examples of street food in Tangier include *caliente* (a shallow circular flan made with chickpea flour and eggs, which was probably introduced by Sephardic Jews), *brik* (a crispy pastry filled with a whole egg and ground meat or tuna), and *Caracoles Tanger* (snails in bowls of spiced soup).

Other locations nearby: 20, 23, 25, 28, 29

25 The Weavers of Tangier

Ville Nouvelle (New City), Fondouk Chejra at the foot of Escalier Waller on Rue Amerique du Sud

Look at an old map of Tangier's Medina and you might see somewhere the word *fondouk* (alternatively *funduq* or *fendak*). It signifies a caravanserai (a combined inn and warehouse), where visiting merchants offloaded their produce for market and spent the night. Several such facilities were once clustered outside the Medina's main gate (Bab al-Fahs) (see no. 12).

You will not see caravans arriving at the Medina today unfortunately, and most of the *fondouks* have vanished with them. Two, however, have survived inside the Medina albeit now repurposed. The early-19th century Fondouk Siaghine at 58 Rue Siaghine comprises, as was typical, a central courtyard for pack animals surrounded by two-storey colonnaded galleries. The ground floor would originally have contained storerooms, with accommodation for the merchants above. The English travel writer George Borrow (1803–1881) noted that silks from Fez could be purchased here, as well as traditional Moroccan slippers *(babouches)* and goods imported from Europe. Today both floors contain clothing shops. By contrast, the 17th century Fendak Dar Dbagh is a roofless shell that today houses stalls promoting local products made by women's co-operatives, as well as a good café.

Another example is the Fondouk Chejra located outside the Medina on Rue Amerique du Sud. It is also known as Fondouk Waller because of its proximity to the Escalier Waller, a flight of stairs popular with streetsellers, which features in the James Bond film *Spectre*. The stairs are named after Ernest Waller (1868–1946), a Yorkshireman who arrived in Tangier in 1893 and set up a real estate company. He facilitated the construction of the Fondouk Chejra to house merchants coming down from the Rif Mountains. Like the Fondouk Siaghine, it had storerooms on the ground floor and sleeping rooms above. Moroccan storyteller Mohamed Choukri (1935–2003) stated in his autobiographical work *For Bread Alone* (1972) that as a poor illiterate he was allowed to sleep at the Fondouk Chejra for just one Spanish peseta a night (Choukri's book is important because it provides a stark corrective to the colonial-era view of Tangier as a glamorous, bohemian playground).

The courtyard of the Fondouk Chejra today has been roofed over and a variety of food and household goods' stalls occupy the ground floor. Upstairs a dozen of the 40 former bedrooms now house the workshops of the city's weavers' co-operative. Here one can see traditional wooden looms in action, with weavers using foot pedals to move the frame, passing the shuttle from side to side by hand. Using rough sheep's wool, cotton, and *sabra* (a shiny silk-like synthetic thread), they make blankets, towels *(fouthas)*, hooded *djel-labas*, slippers, scarves, table mats, and curtains. It is little wonder that French fashion designer Yves Saint Laurent (1936–2008) came here during his time in the city.

A traditional loom in action at the Fondouk Chejra

Tangier is gaining a name for its new breed of female fabric creatives. They include Marie-Laure Godinot, who creates small-batch collections of home linens and women's clothing in her Au Fil de Tanger workshop at 26 Rue Ibn Abbou (Kasbah). Next door is Dar al-Drazz (House of Silk), where Douae La Hrir and her mother work a traditional wooden loom in a tiny workshop (see page 2). Kenza Bennani has set up her *New Tangier* label at 6 Rue Imam Soufiane Taouri (Marshan) and the renowned French-Moroccan entrepreneur Yto Barrada (b. 1961) has created the Mothership, a natural dye garden and traditional weaving workshop up on the Old Mountain (see no. 40).

Tangier is also known for its wicker workers, who skilfully weave baskets, bags, lampshades, and parasols from flax, straw, jute, and rattan. Le Vendeur de Paniers at 45 Rue Gorna (Kasbah) offers a decent selection.

Other locations nearby: 20, 23, 24, 28, 29

26 The German Waterfront

Ville Nouvelle (New City), the Renschhausen Buildings on Avenue Mohammed VI between Rue de la Plage and Rue du Portugal

The presence of Europeans in Tangier during the city's time as an International Zone (1925–1956) has been described as an example of 'Collective Colonialism'. Unlike previous colonial adventures, when a single country held the reins of power, the presence of multiple foreign actors has left an indelible impression on the urban landscape, one that even the removal of colonial-era street names has failed to erase.

Until the early-20th century, Tangier was essentially a medieval Moroccan city, the walled Medina. 'Collective Colonialism' prompted the creation of a new city beyond the Medina's gates, one with distinct districts laid out by the various incoming communities. This modern planned cityscape, with its distinctly European appearance, contrasts strongly with the labyrinthine alleys of the Medina (see nos. 12, 31).

This New City, or Ville Nouvelle, germinated in several locations and often on land that had previously been sand dunes. A French quarter, for example, grew up around the Place de France, where the French Consulate, Gran Café de Paris, Delacroix Gallery, and Lycée

The Renschhausen Buildings with the walled Medina beyond

Regnault are all located today (see no. 29). Similarly, a Spanish quarter developed around Rue de Velázquez (now Rue Khalid Ibn El Oualid), with the Gran Teatro Cervantes as its cultural focal point (see no. 28).

The situation regarding the Germans was somewhat different. German merchants, diplomats, doctors, and civil engineers appeared in the city from 1873 onwards, when a German Embassy was established. One of the engineers was Adolf Renschhausen (1867–1948), who in 1905 secured valuable contracts to expand the Port of Tangier. With the proceeds he developed the nearby waterfront between Rue de la Plage and Rue du Portugal, along what is today, Avenue Mohammed VI. The result, completed in 1913, was called the Renschhausen Buildings.

The Renschhausen Buildings were grandiose by Moroccan standards. Overlooking the sea was a long, four-storey structure notable for its neo-Baroque decoration. In its original iteration, the building had two large stonework crowns at roof level in honour of Kaiser Wilhelm II, and a central panel proclaiming Renschhausen's involvement. The ground floor was taken up with shipping offices (one still retains its four destination boards on the façade), import-export companies, insurance agencies, and banks. Together with the three storeys above occupied by the Hotel Majestic, all made their money from the port.

On the slope behind the hotel, the Renschhausen Terrace was built. This consisted of a balustraded public terrace and another elaborately-decorated neo-Baroque building known as the French Kursaal, which housed a concert hall and casino. This, however, was a later addition made in the early-1920s. Today it houses the Café Cultural Renschhausen, which has several old photos of the place hanging on its walls.

With the outbreak of the First World War in 1914, German influence in Tangier came to an end. German residents were sent to camps in Algeria and Adolf Renschhausen was convicted of spying. Thereafter, the French and Spanish governments bought up German-built properties at auction, including the Renschhausen Buildings, which the Spanish touted as a symbol of Germany's expulsion from Morocco. At the same time the road was named Avenida España and horse races were staged along the sands from here as far as Malabata. Well into the 1950s, the long beach at Tangier was considered one of the world's best.

In 1949, the Renschhausen Buildings were sold to private developers. Today they contain private residences, with restaurants, cafés, and shops at pavement level. The Kursaal had already closed by this time following a ban on gambling and is today a hotel, with retail outlets on the first floor.

Other locations nearby: 4, 7, 8, 9, 27

27 The Old Port Reinvented

Ville Nouvelle (New City), a tour of the Old Port of Tangier including the former Customs House (Al-Diwana) on Place Bab el-Marsa below the Hotel Continental

During the 1970s, the author was taken on holiday to Tangier by his parents. Barely a teenager, he remembers vividly the sight of the Old Port, with its rusty freighters, quayside cranes, and warehouses. Fast forward half a century and the view is unrecognisable. There is still a ferry terminal and a fishermen's dock but the old cargo port has made way for the six-lane Avenue Mohammed VI and Morocco's first urban marina. The changes are all part of the ambitious Tangier City Port redevelopment project instigated by current King Mohammed VI (b. 1963) to help bring Tangier into the 21st century.

Nestled in the Strait of Gibraltar, Tangier has long been known as the Gateway to Africa. The Portuguese realised Tangier's strategic importance but it was left to the English to build the first port, when Tangier was ceded to them in 1662. To make the most out of his new colony, King Charles II (1630–1685) declared Tangier open to free trade and constructed a 740-foot-long seawall to shelter visiting merchant vessels. The project was short-lived though and, when the English departed in 1684, they deliberately left the seawall in ruins.

Tangier was repopulated by Muslims but the seawall was not rebuilt until the late-19th century and then only in the form of a wooden pier. Modifications continued into the first half of the 20th century, when the huge seawall seen today was constructed stretching over half a mile out to sea. It was used for cargo ships until 2007, when port activities were relocated to the huge new Tanger Med Port in Oued Rmel, 25 miles east of Tangier. This vast deep-water facility is currently the largest port in Africa and the Mediterranean.

Much of the Old Port today has been transformed into a new, mixed-use waterfront development called the Tanja Bay Marina replete with 1,400 moorings and row-upon-row of smart apartment complexes. Those who miss the shabby but characterful Tangier of old cite it as an example of how the city is being reinvented at the cost of its Bohemian reputation. Fortunately for them, however, there are still three locations that speak of the past.

First is the Customs House (Al-Diwana) on Place Bab el-Marsa. Built in 1881 close by the Bab el-Hira, one of two gates connecting the Port with the Medina, this distinctive structure with its four ornately-stuccoed arches is where visiting merchant vessels would have their

A view of the Old Port including the Port Mosque

papers checked and cargoes assessed for customs. Old photographs of the building show it surrounded by wooden crates, barrels, and heavily-laden donkeys on their way to market. Now restored, it is home to the Port Centre, a museum and exhibition space that tells the story of the Old Port in images and artefacts.

The second location is Tangier's old main railway station between Rue de la Plage and Rue du Portugal. Opened in 1925, the railway brought passengers and freight directly into the port until the new port opened. With the tracks lifted and the building now the administration centre for the marina, a new railway station has opened farther inland (see no. 49).

The third location, north of the Customs House, is the Lalla Abla Mosque, which overlooks the ferry terminal and Fish Dock. Known as the Port Mosque, the current structure, which supercedes an earlier mosque on the same site, was dedicated by the current king in 2018 in honour of his grandmother, Princess Lalla Abla bint Tahar (1909–1992). It can accommodate 1,900 worshippers in segregated prayer rooms.

Other locations nearby: 8, 9, 10, 11, 12

28 The Gran Teatro Cervantes

Ville Nouvelle (New City), the Gran Teatro Cervantes on Rue Anoual (note: currently closed pending restoration)

Given that Spain lies nine short miles away across the Strait of Gibraltar, it is no surprise that the country has played a significant part in the story of Tangier. As early as 1786, it opened a consulate in the city to facilitate trade, and in 1861 established its own postal service. During the 1880s, Spanish Franciscans built the Church of the Immaculate Conception to serve the city's mostly-Spanish Catholic community. Still the only church in the Medina, it is today used by Saint Teresa's Missionaries of Charity (see no. 37).

From 1912 until 1956, when Morocco gained independence, Tangier was surrounded on its landward side by the Spanish North Moroccan Protectorate. The city itself, from 1925 onwards, was administered by Spain together with a dozen other foreign powers. The Spanish established their own quarter centred on the aptly-named Rue de Velázquez (now Rue Khalid Ibn El Oualid) and Rue Esperanza Orellana (now Rue Anoual). The quarter's focal point was the Gran Teatro Cervantes.

Dedicated to Miguel de Cervantes Saavedra (1547–1616), author of the pioneering novel *Don Quixote*, the theatre was financed by one Don Manuel Peña, and his land-owning wife, Esperanza Orellana.

Ceramic decoration on the Gran Teatro Cervantes

Wealthy members of Spanish-Tanjawi high society, they commissioned the Spanish architect Diego Jiménez Armstrong (1884–1956) to draw up an elegant modernist design, which was realised in reinforced concrete by the Spanish company Construcciones Hidráulicas. The best Spanish craftsmen were employed, including engineer José Gomendio, carpenter José de la Rosa, and artist Federico Ribera, who painted the ceiling. The elaborate sets were the work of the Venetian set designer, Giorgio Busato (1836-1916).

There is no denying in which year the theatre opened since the date '1913' is clearly incorporated into the glorious Art Nouveau tiled façade by Spanish ceramicist Cándido Mata Cañamaque. Just prior to the official inauguration, the 1912 Italian version of the film *Quo Vadis* was screened. The first real cinematic blockbuster, it boasted lavish sets, 5,000 extras, and a running time of two hours. Thereafter, all manner of productions were staged at the theatre, including not only plays and opera but also Spanish lyric-dramas *(zarzuelas)* and programmes of Andalusian poetic songs *(coplas)*. The first 'talkie' in Tangier was screened here in 1929.

With a maximum capacity of 1,400 spectators, the Gran Teatro Cervantes was for many years the largest and most successful theatrical venue in North Africa. As such, it attracted many renowned performers, including Enrico Caruso (1873–1921) and Sarah Bernhardt (1844–1923), Cuban *bolerista* Antonio Machín (1903–1977), Argentinian crooner Carlos Gardel (1890–1935), and Mexican singer Jorge Negete (1911–1953), who rode onto the stage on a white horse!

In 1929, the theatre was bequeathed to the Spanish Government, which eventually sold it in 1974 to the City of Tangier for a symbolic one Dirham. By this point the running costs had become onerous and the Tangier International Zone (1925–1956) had long since ended. The theatre closed and fell into disrepair until 2016, when plans were put in motion to restore it for use as a cultural centre. Today, it is once again a sight to behold.

A less well-known Spanish relic is the former Dox Monopolio tobacco factory near the roundabout on Avenue Oujda (Ville Nouvelle). Built by Juan March Ordinas (1880–1962), the wealthiest man in Spain at the time, who monopolised tobacco production during the time of the Spanish North Moroccan Protectorate, the quaint villa-like building is today stranded amidst more modern structures.

Other locations nearby: 24, 25, 28, 29, 30, 31

29 At the Gran Café de Paris

Ville Nouvelle (New City), the Gran Café de Paris on the Place de France

Tangier has a renowned and well-established café culture. Coffee first arrived in Morocco during the 16th century along trade routes that connected the Middle East with Europe. By the 18th century, coffee shops known as *qahwa* began appearing. Later, during the time of the Tangier International Zone (1925–1956), when the city was administered by various foreign powers, several European-style cafés were established in the Ville Nouvelle (New City) to satisfy the growing number of expatriates. With the exception of Madame Porte's on Avenue Prince Moulay Abdellah, which is now a branch of MacDonald's (the original neon sign remains), most are still in business (see no. 6).

The *Grand Dame* of historic cafés is undoubtedly the Gran Café de Paris, which was founded in 1927 and run by a Madame Leontine. Located on the Place de France (Ville Nouvelle), its Gallic name reflects the presence opposite of the French Consulate, which opened a year later. An extension to the café in the 1950s garnered it the epithet 'Gran'. The surrounding area was the first part of the Ville Nouvelle to be developed outside the Medina. It is remarkable to think that at the time much of the area was sand dunes (see no. 31)!

The corner location of the Gran Café de Paris dictates its ambience both inside and out. Outside, a crescent of chairs is popular with locals, who come to chat, smoke, and drink *Thé de Menthe* (mint tea) or strong *Café Marocaine* despite the busy traffic. The spacious interior is calmer, with clusters of comfortable leather armchairs facing matching banquettes. The high ceilings, fluted pillars, and decorative wood panelling add a touch of elegance, as do the waiters in their white shirts and black waistcoats. One could almost be in a coffeehouse in Vienna were it not for the respectful framed photo of the Moroccan king.

For almost a century now the Gran Café de Paris has been a place to linger. Habitués of note have included the American author Paul Bowles (1910–1999), who spent much of his life in Tangier, and his compatriot, the Beat Generation writer and visual artist William Burroughs (1914–1997), who wrote *The Naked Lunch* (1959) in the city. Others known to have passed through include James Bond author Ian Fleming (1908–1964), photographer and costumier Cecil Beaton (1904–1980), Spanish poet Juan Goytisolo (1931–2017), and writers Samuel Beckett (1906–1989), Tennessee Williams (1911–1983), Jean Genet (1910–1986), and Antoine de Saint-Exupéry (1900–1944). The Moroccan storytellers Mohamed Choukri (1935–2003) and Larbi Layachi (1937–1986) were also here. More recently the café achieved celluloid fame when it provided the backdrop for a scene in the action-thriller film *The Bourne Ultimatum* (2007).

Lazy hours at the Gran Café de Paris

Younger Tanjawis are sometimes irritated by visitors viewing their city solely through a nostalgic 20th century lens. They are heartened by the fact that Tangier's traditional café culture is now being supplemented with more modern establishments. Typical is Alma Kitchen and Coffee at 44 Rue Antaki and Crumby at 2 Rue de Grenade (both Ville Nouvelle), which manage to be Moroccan without recourse to the traditional or the exotic. Another is Le Salon Bleu, which despite its historic location overlooking Place de la Kasbah, manages a contemporary ambience, with good Moroccan mezze of olives, hummus, and *zaalouk* (grilled aubergine with tomatoes).

Other locations nearby: 23, 24, 25, 28

30 Street of the Beats

Ville Nouvelle (New City), the Hotel Muniria and TangerInn at 1 Rue Magellan

Between 1925 and 1956, Tangier was an International Zone, where Berbers, Moroccans, and Gulf Arabs co-existed alongside Europeans and Americans. Tolerance was required on all sides and it was this permissiveness that attracted the colourful expatriates still associated with the city today.

Alongside the spies, smugglers, adventurers, and socialites were the Beats, a group of authors who explored and liberalised North American culture after the Second World War. The main tenets of their work were the abandonment of standard narrative values, the rejection of economic materialism, explicit portrayals of the human condition, experimentation with psychedelic drugs, and sexual liberation.

The Villa Muniria where William Burroughs wrote The Naked Lunch

The three best-known Beat works are *The Naked Lunch* (1959) by William Burroughs (1914–1997), *On the Road* (1957) by Jack Kerouac (1922–1969), and *Howl* (1956) by Allen Ginsberg (1926–1997). All three first met in 1944 in New York City and it was in Tangier during the 1950s that they regrouped. Fleeing the restrictions of McCarthyism, they made Tangier a beacon of freedom for nonconformists.

Unlike the city's well-to-do expats, who gravitated towards the leafy slopes of the Old Mountain, the Beats congregated on a side street in the Ville Nouvelle (New City). Rue Magellan runs from Boulevard Pasteur down towards the waterfront. At the top of the street stands the Hotel Rembrandt, where in 1954 Burroughs befriended fellow Beat Brion Gysin (1916–1986), who was exhibiting his abstract desert paintings inspired by trips taken with the writer Paul Bowles (1910–1999) (see no. 38). At the time Gysin also ran the 1001 Nights restaurant, where he hired the Master Musicians of Jajouka to perform their trancelike music in a wing of the whitewashed Menebhi Palace on Rue Assad Ibn al Farrat (Marshan), once home to the sultan's Minister of Defence. Later, in 1959, he pioneered his 'cut-up' technique, a method of writing that involved slicing up newspaper text and reassembling it in a random order. Burroughs would put the technique to good use in his own work during the early 1960s.

The principal address for the Beats, however, stands at the foot of Rue Magellan. The Hotel Muniria at number 1, with its basement bar the TangerInn (sic), is where Burroughs, Kerouac, and Ginsberg all stayed during the 1950s. Burroughs, the first to arrive, in 1954, stayed initially on the top floor and later moved down to the ground floor. Living in squalor, it was here that he weaned himself off hard drugs and wrote *Interzone*, the 'antinovel' that became *The Naked Lunch*. The title was suggested by Kerouac, who lodged briefly at the Muniria in early 1957 whilst awaiting proofs of his own novel *The Subterraneans* (1959). Burroughs' former lover Ginsberg arrived at the Muniria shortly afterwards to help organise the first draft of *The Naked Lunch*. The scene of both creativity and craziness, it is no surprise that the Beats nicknamed the Muniria the Villa Delirium!

Most of the bars frequented by the Beats and their contemporaries are long gone. They included the Blue Parrot, Grillon, Les Liaisons, Mar Chica, Navarra, Parade, Safari, and Windmill. Most famous was Dean's at 2 Rue Amerique du Sud (Ville Nouvelle). The eponymous Dean (thought to be former London underworld figure, Donald Kimfull, under the assumed name of Joseph Dean) was originally head bartender at the El Minzah Hotel before opening his own bar in 1937 (see no. 9). Until his death in 1962 from a cocaine overdose, he welcomed everyone from Errol Flynn (1909–1959) and Ava Gardner (1922–1990) to Noël Coward (1899–1973), Ian Fleming (1908–1964), and Francis Bacon (1909–1992).

Other locations nearby: 28, 29, 31, 32

31 A City from the Sand

Ville Nouvelle (New City), a European architecture tour including the Casa de España at 47 Boulevard Pasteur

The first Western diplomats arrived in Tangier during the 18th century. They set up their consulates inside the Medina (Old City), protected from Berber attack by walls erected two centuries earlier by the Portuguese. During the 19th century, this diplomatic presence facilitated improved sanitation (1879), a printing press (1880), and Morocco's first telephone (1883). It was not until the early years of the 20th century, however, that population growth necessitated the creation of a new city, the Ville Nouvelle, beyond the walls of the Medina.

The first roads in the Ville Nouvelle fanned out from the Grand Socco, the unpaved area immediately outside the Medina, where caravans traditionally offloaded their wares for market. They included Rue d'Italie, which ran northwards towards the Marshan, Rue d'Espagne eastwards to the port, Rue d'Angleterre to the west, and Rue de la Liberté, which led south onto Boulevard Pasteur. The European street names are telling and along them Western-style architecture emerged in a variety of styles.

Boulevard Pasteur, which was laid out in 1910, is still the Ville Nouvelle's main thoroughfare. Before that, however, two interesting buildings had appeared on land which at the time was still sand dunes. The first was the Catholic Mission of Sagrado Corazón de Jesús (1907). Still standing at Rue Al Jabha al Watania 2, it was designed by the Spanish Franciscan architect Francisco Serra Linares (1866–1930). Its location garnered it the nickname Iglesia de las Arenas (Church of the Sands). It is used today for charitable purposes. The second was the Dar es-Salaf (House of Debt) (1910) at 29 Boulevard Pasteur, where port taxes were collected to pay off French war debts. Rendered in the Hispano-Moorish style, it provided the street with its original name, Boulevard de la Dette, before the more fashionable 'Boulevard Pasteur' was introduced. It today houses the Regional Tourism Authority.

The first real development occurred around the Place de France. The French Consulate and Gran Café de Paris were both installed here during the 1920s making it the hub of French activity in the city (the British, Germans, Italians, and Spanish all had their hubs too) (see nos 21, 26, 28, 29, 36). The Boulevard Pasteur ('Le Boulevard'), which runs south-east from here to join Avenue Mohammed V, is lined with Beaux Arts and Art Deco buildings of the same period. Despite the French connection, however, much of the work was done by Spanish developers, namely the Toledano family, in conjunction with the Tanjawi bourgeoisie. Their favoured architect was Paris-trained Spanish architect Diego Jiménez Armstrong (1884-1956), whose balconied apartment blocks, with shops at pavement level, are easy to spot, as are his elegant whitewashed villas. One of these, at number 27, contains Tangier's sole working synagogue. The addition of cafés and hotels soon made the boulevard the fashionable centre of Tangier.

The Casa de España on Boulevard Pasteur

During the early 1950s, when Tangier was still an International Zone, the boulevard saw the construction of two tall corner buildings at its southern end. The Rationalist-style Casa de España at number 47 is again the work of Diego Jiménez Armstrong, whereas its counterpart across the road, the Expressionist-style Goicoechea building, is the work of Manuel Martínez Chumillas (1902–1986).

Boulevard Pasteur is named for the French chemist, pharmacist, and microbiologist Louis Pasteur (1822–1895). The presence in Morocco of the Pasteur Institute of Paris dates back to 1911, when a branch was established on Rue Qortobi Marchane (Marshan).

Other locations nearby: 28, 29, 30, 32

32 The Librairie des Colonnes

Ville Nouvelle (New City), the Librairie des Colonnes at 54 Boulevard Pasteur

Tangier's literary heritage encompasses the 15th century *Travels* of Ibn Battouta (1304–1368/1369 or 1377), the works of 1950s and 60s Beat Generation authors such as William Burroughs (1914–1997), and modern Tanjawi storytellers such as Mohamed Mrabet (b. 1936) and Larbi Layachi (1937–1986).

For the last three quarters of a century, the literary heart of Tangier has been the Librairie des Colonnes at 54 Boulevard Pasteur (Ville Nouvelle). Opened in 1949 as a paper shop, it was acquired in 1951 by French publisher Gallimard as a showcase for its publications. Thereafter it was run as a combined literary salon and art gallery by the Gérofis, a family of Belgian literature enthusiasts. In 2009, the shop was acquired by Pierre Bergé (1930–2017), onetime partner of fashion designer Yves Saint Laurent (1936–2008), and it was subsequently owned by Moroccan businessman and art collector Fadel Iraki.

Bookseller Moncef Bouali at Librairie des Colonnes

The Librairie des Colonnes is not a large store and yet its cedarwood shelves manage to carry considerable weight – from classic literature and poetry to modern novels and philosophical treatises, and in several languages, too. This reflects the international appeal of a city where five languages can be heard: *Darija* (a vernacular Arab dialect spoken in the Maghreb), Berber, French, Spanish, and English.

In addition to selling books, the shop has long served as a meeting place for local and international writers, artists, and intellectuals. André Gide (1869–1951) and Jack Kerouac (1922–1969) came for inspiration, Paul Bowles (1910–1999) and Jean Genet (1910–1986) used it as a cash counter for advance payments and a *poste restante* respectively, and Moroccan storyteller Mohamed Choukri (1935–2003) was a regular in the reading room. Others who came included Irish author Samuel Beckett (1906–1989), the Americans Tennessee Williams (1911–1983) and Truman Capote (1924–1984), Spanish poet Juan Goytisolo (1931–2017), Frenchman Paul Morand (1888–1976), and the Moroccan Tahar Ben Jelloun (b. 1944).

With its distinctive red-columned façade that gives the shop its name and long-standing programme of readings, debates, and art exhibitions, the Librairie des Colonnes has preserved its original charm whilst also embracing modern bookselling. It has also become a key player in the city's cultural life along with international institutions such as the Institut Français, Goethe Institute, Instituto Cervantes, and Palais des Institutions Italiennes. Perhaps most importantly, it has done much to promote the work of homegrown authors to an audience far beyond the borders of Morocco.

In the wake of the reputation established by the Librairie des Colonnes other bookshops have been established. They include Les Insolites around the corner at 28 Khalid Ibn El Oualid, which opened in 2010. Here can be found a carefully-curated mix of Maghrebi- and Mediterranean-interest books, and designer stationery, supplemented by art exhibitions, and other cultural activities. Another is Le Cercle des Arts at 40 Rue Antaki, near the Place des Nations, which has the added attraction of a café and a theatre. Other bookshops include La Virgule Jaune at 26 Rue Moussa Ben Noussair, Librairie Papeterie Marocaine at 3 Rue de Fès, and the Librairie Grand Socco.

Of particular interest is Interzone at 43 Rue Ahmed Ben Ajiba (Kasbah). The brainchild of Danish-Moroccan owner Jonas Senhadji, this unique address is not only a shop selling books, posters, postcards, and music celebrating the period of the Tangier International Zone (1925–1956) but also a museum of artefacts relating to the period. Above the cash register can be seen the original nameplate from the legendary Dean's Bar and around the door are black-and-white caricatures of Tangier celebrities painted by street artist Punksy.

Other locations nearby: 28, 29, 30, 31

33 Carthaginians and Romans

Inner Suburbs: Marshan, the Phoenician Necropolis at Gharsa Ghanam off Avenue Hadj Mohamed Tazi (note: the necropolis is open all hours)

Around 1000 BC, Phoenician traders from the Levant were active in the Tangier region. They were followed in the 5th century BC by the Carthaginians, who kick-started the city's long colonial history by establishing the trading post of Tingis. Later, in 82 BC, Tingis was annexed by the Romans as Colonia Iulia Tingi, which became a part of their province of Mauretania Tingitana. Although the Romans abandoned their North African ambitions in AD 285, Morocco remained a part of the Roman Empire until AD 429.

Despite such a long history of occupation centred solely on the Medina (Old City), there are surprisingly few tangible remains from these early times. To see anything substantial one must stray beyond the walls into the Marshan, where a plateau called Gharsa Ghanam is the site of a Carthaginian (Punic) necropolis. It can be reached from the Bab el-Kasbah by following Rue Assad Ibn al Farrat and Avenue Hadj Mohamed Tazi. Alternatively, and more dramatically, it can be accessed from the Corniche coast road (Route de la Plage Merkala) by means of a rock-cut staircase that traverses the sea cliffs.

Excavated between 1910 and 1960, the necropolis consisted of 98 tombs, half of which were cut into the bedrock. Of these 20 or so are visible today overlooking the blue-and-white Marshan Mosque (Jami' al-Marshan) below (see back cover). Grave goods discovered by archaeologists dating the site to the 5th and 4th centuries BC are displayed in the Kasbah Museum alongside Phoenician artefacts (see no. 17). A similar set of rock-cut tombs, some with their roof slabs intact, can be found on Rue Imam Ibn Hanbal several streets to the south.

Of the Romans there is also little to see. Continuous occupation of the Medina has meant that Roman Tangier has defied excavation. A few shadowy remains and informed guesswork, however, have enabled archaeologists to recreate the town's basic elements. The fortifications protecting the Medina, for example, which were built during the Portuguese-era (1471–1661), most likely sit atop the remains of Roman walls. Rue Siaghine and Rue de la Marine, the main west–east streets that run through the Petit Socco to the Old Port, lie over the Roman *Decumanus Maximus*. Likewise, the Rue des Almohades corresponds with the north–south Roman *Cardo Maximus*. Both streets are standard features of a Roman town. Additionally, the scant outlines of

The Phoenician Necropolis at Gharsa Ghanam

a bath house have been identified beneath the Kasbah, and the Kasbah Museum contains various Roman inscriptions, mosaic fragments, as well as wall paintings from the Bou Kachkach Roman necropolis south of the Medina.

We also know that the Grand Mosque (Jami' al-Kebir) on Rue de la Marine occupies the site of a Roman temple dedicated to Hercules and that the Petit Socco occupies the site of the Roman forum. This juxtaposition of holy place and market would become the norm in the later medieval medinas of Morocco (see no. 6).

To better appreciate the Romans, visit the site of Lixus near Larache, 50 miles south of Tangier. The ruins here include temples, baths, and the remains of a factory for the preparation of *garum*, a popular but pungent fermented fish sauce. Megalithic remains here make Lixus one of the oldest sites in Morocco. Another *garum* factory has been identified at Cotta, a Roman site just south of the Caves of Hercules, although it is unfortunately not accessible as it lies on land belonging to a Saudi Arabian prince (hence the helipad!). Finds from both sites are displayed in the Kasbah Museum in Tangier.

Other locations nearby: 34, 35, 36

34 Kif with Keith

Inner Suburbs: Marshan, Café Hafa at the end of Rue Hafa (note: the café gets busy in the high season)

Café Baba is one of the storied cafés of Tangier. Located on Rue Sidi Hassani in the northern reaches of the Medina, it opened in 1943. Part of its fame stems from a pair of photos on the wall. One shows Keith Richards of the Rolling Stones, who was born the same year, holding a drug-filled pipe (back then the place was called Abdelkader's Kif Café). The other shows the late celebrity chef and fellow libertarian Anthony Bourdain (1956–2018). Their presence helped put the café on the map, and reinforced the image of smoking drugs as an act of pleasurable rebellion.

Morocco's three main recreational drugs are *hashish*, *kif*, and *majoun*. *Hashish* (meaning 'dried herb' in Arabic) is resin made from the female Cannabis plant (known also as marijuana or hemp), which is powdered and pressed into cakes. *Kif* ('pleasure') is made from the potent dried flowers of the female Cannabis plant, which are chopped, mixed with tobacco, and smoked in a small-bowled clay pipe called a *sebsi*. *Majoun* ('kneaded' or 'paste') is a ball-shaped confection made by mixing *kif* with butter, chocolate, dried

Café Hafa and its famous sea view

fruit, nuts, honey, and spices. Despite all three products being illegal in Morocco, cannabis cultivation is officially tolerated in an area of 60 square miles in the high Rif Mountains, where it constitutes the main cash crop of local farmers.

Keith Richards' trip to Tangier is well documented. In February 1967, together with Brian Jones (1942–1969) and his girlfriend, Anita Pallenberg (1942–2017), he set off in a chauffeuer-driven Bentley. By the time they arrived at the El Minzah Hotel, where they were joined by Mick Jagger (b. 1943), Brian was out of the picture with pneumonia, and Keith had fallen for Anita. Brian arrived later and together with Keith and Anita bought large quantities of drugs from a dealer named Achmed Hamifsah (see no. 24). They were also introduced to artist and inventor Brion Gysin (1916–1986), who pioneered the 'cut-up' technique, as well as writer Paul Bowles (1910–1999), although he had little idea who they were!

During a subsequent trip a year later, Brian and new girlfriend Suki Potier (1947–1981) visited the village of Jajouka in the foothills of the Rif Mountains. There Brian recorded local musicians playing time-honoured Sufi trance music, which was released as *Brian Jones Presents Pipes of Pan at Jajouka* (1971). They also visited Café Hafa on the sea cliffs of the Marshan (the word *hafa* means 'cliff'). Opened as a drinking den called La Guinguette Fleurie in 1921 by an elderly Frenchman, this is the oldest café in Tangier and consists of little more than a series of whitewashed terraces furnished with cheap tables and chairs. The real attraction is the dreamy, far-reaching view across the Strait of Gibraltar to Spain. Mint tea, the national drink of Morocco, is the drink of choice, served hot and very sweet. Other musicians associated with Café Hafa include Jimi Hendrix (1942–1970), Patti Smith (b. 1946), and the Beatles.

The Stones returned to Tangier in 1989 to record their song *Continental Drift* with the Master Musicians of Jajouka led by Bachir Attar. The venue was the Palais Akaaboune at 32 Rue Ibn Abbou (Kasbah), a beautiful private residence that can be seen in the James Bond film *Spectre* (2015).

Tangier's second oldest café is Café Porto Rico at 21 Rue de la Plage (Ville Nouvelle). This hole-in-the-wall establishment opened in 1924 and is still in the same hands. The speciality is coffee made with house-roasted Brazilian beans mixed with a unique blend of spices.

Other locations nearby: 33, 35, 36

35 Malcolm Forbes' Toy Soldiers

Inner Suburbs: Marshan, the Mendoub's Residence (Dar al-Mandub) at the junction of Avenue Hadj Mohamed Tazi and Rue Shakespeare (note: the property can only be viewed from the outside)

The Marshan neighbourhood covers the plateau immediately west of the Kasbah. Residential settlement began here around 1840, notably by Europeans looking for a peaceful life away from the commotion of the Medina. Just ten minutes' walk from the city centre and with sweeping sea views, the Marshan remains a sought-after place to live.

One of the Marshan's finest properties is the Mendoub's Residence (Dar al-Mandub) located at the junction of Avenue Hadj Mohamed Tazi and Rue Shakespeare. It was built in 1929, during the time of the Tangier International Zone (1925–1956), when the governance of the city's majority Muslim and Jewish communities was entrusted to a personal representative of the Sultan known as the *Mendoub*. The building should not be confused with the Mendoub's office, the Mendoubia Palace (Dar Mandubiya) on the Grand Socco (see no. 19).

Between 1913 and 1954, the roles of *Naib* (the sultan's intermediary prior to the time of the Tangier International Zone) and then *Mendoub* were fulfilled by the same man: Mohammed Tazi (d. 1954). He commissioned the Mendoub's Residence in 1929. Only

The former Mendoub's Residence owned later by Malcolm Forbes

during the Spanish occupation of Tangier between 1940 and 1945 was he absent from the city.

With Moroccan independence in 1956, the role of Mendoub became obsolete. Later, in 1970, the former Mendoub's Residence was purchased by the American publishing magnate, Malcolm Forbes (1919–1990). Known for his extravagance, he held his 70th birthday party here, jetting in 800 guests, including Henry Kissinger, Calvin Klein, and actress Elizabeth Taylor. Entertainment was provided by 600 drummers, 400 belly dancers, and 300 Berber horsemen!

Forbes converted part of the building into a public museum in which he installed his remarkable collection of 115,000 model tin soldiers. In a series of showcases, he recreated famous battles from Waterloo (1815) to Diên Biên Phu (1954), with lighting and sound effects to add atmosphere. Some of the models can be seen in the James Bond film *The Living Daylights* (1987). In the garden there were 600 figures representing the Battle of the Three Kings (known locally as the Battle of Wadi al-Makhāzin), which took place in 1578 at Ksar el-Kebir, south of Tangier. A victory for Sultan Abd al-Malik I (1541–1578), it marked an end to Portuguese attempts to reconquer territories it had lost in Morocco. Following Forbes' death, some of the soldiers found their way to the American Legation Museum in the Medina (see no. 4). The rest of the collection was auctioned off and the building became a government residence for visiting dignitaries.

Directly opposite the Mendoub's Residence is the Marshan Palace built in the 1950s as the seat of the Legislative Assembly of the International Zone. Today, the building serves as a venue for diplomatic events and it was here in 2015 that King Mohammed VI (b. 1963) met with French President François Hollande (b. 1954) to discuss climate change. Beyond the palace is the large Sidi Ben Abdessadak Muslim Cemetery named in honour of a prominent Riffian family.

Farther west along Rue Shakespeare is the impressive but crumbling former home of the Scotsman Caid Sir Harry Maclean (1848–1920), who acted as military advisor to several sultans. It was from here in 1907 that he was kidnapped by the Riffian warlord Raisuli and held until the British government paid a ransom (see no. 42).

Mendoub **Mohammed Tazi had a second luxury residence farther west, high above the Rmilat forest. It is today the opulent Fairmont Tazi Palace hotel, which offers a black marble swimming pool and murals by Togolese French graffiti artist Mattia Sitou.**

Other locations nearby: 33, 34, 36, 39

36 The Sultans who Sold Morocco

Inner Suburbs: Iberia (San Francisco), the Palais des Institutions Italiennes (former Abd al-Hafid Palace) on Rue Mohamed Ben Abdelouahab

In 1912, by the terms of the Convention of Fez, control of Morocco was effectively relinquished to the French and Spanish. Morocco would not experience true independence again until 1956. To understand how this situation came about one must consider the reigns of three successive sultans.

The first, Sultan Hassan I (1836–1894), maintained Moroccan independence at a time when Egypt and Tunisia were falling under foreign control. By introducing military and administrative reforms, he increased the power of the Moroccan royal court *(Makhzen)* and received loyalty from powerful tribal chiefs.

During the subsequent reign of Sultan Abd al-Aziz (1878–1943), much of this work was undone. Proclaimed sultan aged just twelve, he implemented a hugely unpopular tax on agriculture and livestock to help finance his extravagant European tastes and hobbies. He also borrowed heavily from the French and the Germans, which encouraged encroachments onto Moroccan territory. In 1905, Kaiser Wilhelm II (1859–1941) visited Tangier and advised the sultan to call a conference to set Moroccan affairs in order. By the terms of the Algeciras Conference (1906), the independence of the Sultanate was respected but Morocco would henceforth be subject to an international protectorate. The country's finances now relied on French, German, British, and Spanish loans, and Europeans received the right to own Moroccan land.

The result was widespread revolt and in 1908 the sultan was deposed in favour of his brother, Abd al-Hafid (1875/1880–1937). Initially opposed to his predecessor's concessions, his signature on the Convention of Fez saw most of Morocco become a French protectorate, with Spain granted northern Morocco to prevent French control of the Strait (Germany received African territories elsewhere and France agreed to stay clear of British-administered Egypt). The carve-up was complete.

Abd al-Hafid lasted just four years. Lured by the promise of an enormous French pension, he abdicated in 1912 and was exiled to Tangier. Initially he installed himself and his retinue of 168 wives, concubines, and servants in the Kasbah. When this proved inadequate, he commissioned a huge palace on Rue Mohamed Ben Abdelouahab (Iberia). It was completed in 1914 to a design in reinforced concrete

The vast Palace of exiled Sultan Abd Al-Hafid

by Spanish architect Diego Jiménez Armstrong (1884-1956), who designed the Teatro Cervantes around the same time (see no. 28). Despite such extravagance, the ex-sultan never lived there and instead spent his time in France and Spain (nor did he use a second palace constructed on the Old Mountain on the former site of Ravensrock, the home of British Envoy Extraordinary to the Moorish Court, Sir John Hay Drummond Hay (1816–1893)).

The palace on Rue Mohamed Ben Abdelouahab remained unused until 1926, when it was auctioned off to the Italian government, which at the time only had a small footprint in the city. By the 1940s an Italian church dedicated to Francis of Assisi had been erected in the grounds together with a school, hospital, post office, and telegraph station. Not to be outdone, the French built their Church of Our Lady of the Assumption (1953) on Rue Ibn Toumert and the Spanish completed their long-delayed Cathedral of the Immaculate Conception and the Holy Spirit (1961) on Avenue Hassan II (see no. 37).

Known today as the Palais des Institutions Italiennes, the old palace contains a hospital run by Franciscan nuns, the office of the Italian vice-consul, and the Casa d'Italia restaurant, which has a terrace opening onto a beautiful central courtyard. There is even a *bocce* ball court in the grounds. In recent years the building has also been used to host cultural events, including the Tanjazz music festival, Tangier International Book Fair, and Tangier Fashion Week 2025.

Other locations nearby: 33, 34, 35, 37, 38

37 The Spire and the Minaret

Inner Suburbs: Iberia (San Francisco), the Cathedral of the Immaculate Conception and the Holy Spirit at the junction of Rue Sidi Bouabid and Avenue Hassan II

During the 1970s, a Kuwaiti sheikh visiting Tangier was displeased by the fact that the spire of the city's Roman Catholic Cathedral dominated the skyline. To rectify the situation, he financed the construction of a mosque with a minaret taller than the spire. Completed in 1983, the Mohammed V Mosque (Jami' Mohammed V) still lays claim to the city's tallest minaret.

Both the cathedral and the mosque are in the Iberia neighbourhood, south-west of the Grand Socco. The unusual name is derived from a large sign advertising the Spanish airline *Iberia* that until recently adorned a building on Place du Koweit. Originally, however, the neighbourhood was called San Francisco in deference to the city's long-standing presence of the Franciscans.

For many years, the only Catholic place of worship in all Morocco was a chapel attached to the Spanish Consulate in Tangier's Medina. This was superceded in 1881 by the Church of the Immaculate Conception on Rue Siaghine. Its construction was overseen by Father José María Lerchundi (1836–1896), who one year later acquired property outside the Medina for a Franciscan convent. Initially just a hospital was built at the junction of Rue Sidi Bouabid (formerly Rue San Francisco) and Avenue Hassan II. Conventual buildings followed designed initially by Spanish architect Antoni Gaudí (1852–1926), who conjured up a spectacular, multi-spired building based on Saharan vernacular architecture. When this proved too expensive, a sobre neo-Renaissance design completed in 1904 was used instead.

Work started on the convent church the same year but progress faltered. Indeed not until the 1940s, when Francoist Spain set about regaining influence in the Tangier International Zone, did building recommence. Spurred on by the fact that both Italy and France had recently built churches, the unfinished Franciscan church project was upgraded to that of a cathedral. Completed in 1961 to a design by Spanish architect Luis Martínez-Feduchi (1901–1975), the Cathedral of the Immaculate Conception and the Holy Spirit is a modern streamlined construction of reinforced concrete, with a light-filled triple-nave, an apse that is as much stained glass as it is wall, and a 157 feet-high spire-topped belfry loosely informed by St. Mark's in Venice. The tomb of Father Lerchundi (1836–1896) lies in the crypt.

The Mohammed V Mosque, with its spire-beating minaret, stands not far away at the junction of Avenue Belgique and Avenue Sidi Mohammed Ben Abdellah. It overlooks the Place du Koweit, named in honour of the country that financed the mosque's construction. The mosque itself is named after Mohammed V (1909–1961), the last sultan and first king of Morocco, who famously spoke up for Moroccan independence in the Mendoubia Gardens in 1947 (see no. 19).

Inside the Cathedral of the Immaculate Conception and the Holy Spirit

Visible from the Strait of Gibraltar when arriving by sea, the mosque is a gem of traditional Moroccan architecture. The magnificent interior features carved stucco arches, a huge carpet, stained glass skylights, and brass candelabra suspended on chains from the roof. The mosque complex also contains a theological school, library, and boarding school, as well as the regional seat of the *Ulama* (a body of scholars with specialist knowledge of Islamic sacred law) and the local seat of the Moroccan Ministry of Habous (Inalienable Charitable Endowments).

Not far from the mosque, at the junction of Rue Sidi Bouarrakia and Avenue Hassan II, is the more modest mosque and mausoleum *(marabout)* of Sidi Bouarrakia (d. 1718), patron saint of Tangier. Greatly admired for his piety and courage in the fight against colonialism, he is venerated with considerable ceremony on the Prophet Muhammad's birthday *(Mawlid)*.

Other locations nearby: 22, 23, 36, 38

38 At Home with Paul Bowles

Inner Suburbs: Iberia (San Francisco), the Immeuble Itesa at 38 Rue Imam Kastalani (note: Paul Bowles' former apartment is private but the entrance to the building can be visited to the rear)

American author, composer, and translator Paul Bowles (1910–1999) was in many ways the quintessential expatriate in Tangier. Wildy creative, sexually ambivalent, a smoker of *kif*, and with a streak of eccentricity (he carried a pet parrot called Babarhio on his shoulder), he was an enigmatic exile who personified the city in the 20th century.

Bowles received a middle-class upbringing in New York City. Despite a cold relationship with his father, his mother nurtured his creative talents. As a young adult he attended the University of Virginia and made several trips to Paris, where he studied music with budding composer Aaron Copland (1900–1990). Back in New York he made a living writing music for piano and theatre productions. Writing literature, however, was always in the back of his mind and in 1947 he received a publisher's contract for a novel. With the advance he relocated to Tangier, where he lived for the rest of his life.

That first novel, *The Sheltering Sky* (1949), was set in French North Africa, which Bowles had visited with Copland in 1931. It is the tale of a married couple from New York, Port and Kit Moresby, who head into the desert to resolve their marital difficulties. Their journey is fraught with dangers and difficulties, all played out beneath the increasingly occluded firmament of the book's title. The book's critical and popular success established Bowles as a major literary force.

A plaque marks the former home of author Paul Bowles

Bowles found Tangier an intriguing place. Exotic, unfamiliar, and multinational, the city had been an International Zone since 1925. The permissiveness necessary for Berbers, Arabs, Europeans, and Americans to live together created an atmosphere in which creatives such as Bowles could work and play. Even after Morocco gained independence in 1956, Tangier remained a city at the edge, where most things were possible.

Bowles' first house in Tangier still stands on the south side of Place Amrah in the Medina. Lacking a bathroom, it did not impress his wife and fellow writer, Jane (1917–1973), who joined him there in 1948. Their open and unorthodox marriage clearly inspired that of Port and Kit in *The Sheltering Sky*.

Paul Bowles' suitcases in the Old American Legation Museum

The property most associated with Bowles, however, is the Immeuble Itesa at 38 Rue Imam Kastalani (Iberia). He moved into a suite of rooms on the top floor of this Italian-style apartment building shortly after its construction in 1959. At the time it was surrounded by scrubby fields of grazing animals, with a distant view of the Strait, but today it is surrounded by buildings. It was here in the lounge, with its rugs, floor cushions, bookcases, and fireplace, that Bowles welcomed his visitors, including William Burroughs (1914–1997), Tennessee Williams (1911–1983), Jack Kerouac (1922–1969), Truman Capote (1924–1984), Patricia Highsmith (1921–1995), Gore Vidal (1925–2012), and Mick Jagger (b. 1943).

Bowles remained at the Immeuble Itesa until two weeks before his death in 1999. The apartment today is private but the public entrance to the rear can be visited. Fortunately, many of Bowles' personal effects are preserved at the Old American Legation Museum in the Medina (see no. 4). There is also one further location where the ghost of Paul Bowles still lingers. In the final scene of Bernardo Bertolucci's film version of *The Sheltering Sky* (1990) Kit returns to Tangier after Port's death. She happens upon the real-life Café Colon on Rue d'Italie, directly opposite the Cine Alcazar, where Bowles himself is sitting (it was one of his favourite cafés). "Are you lost?" he enquires. "Yes" Kit replies with an enigmatic smile.

Other locations nearby: 37, 38

39 Ghosts of Merkala Beach

Outer Suburbs (Old Mountain), Merkala Beach where the Corniche coast road (Route de la Plage Merkala) meets the Route de la Vieille Montagne

In his book *Two Years Beside the Strait* (1990), author Paul Bowles (1910–1999) records Wednesday 19th August 1987 as being a clear day, with a forceful east wind *(cherqi)* blowing off the Sahara. He takes a walk to Merkala Beach, between the Marshan and the Old Mountain, where small children are playing games with strands of seaweed, and there is a strong smell of sewage. The beach today is a very different place. The smell is long gone but so has much of what Bowles would have recognised.

Back in Bowles' day, Merkala Beach was reached by means of the Route de la Vieille Montagne, which snakes its way between the neighbourhoods of Iberia and Dradeb before dropping down to the sea along a river valley. Historians know this valley as the *Oued Lihoud* (Jews' River), as it is said that the Jews landed here after their expulsion from Spain in 1492. It was also here on 3rd May 1662, that a 500-strong Anglo-Irish force suffered heavy losses at the hands of the Moroccan warlord Khadir Ghailan (1599–1673). Two years later almost to the day, the Earl of Teviot suffered an equally ignominious defeat at the same spot. Such attacks led to the English abandonment of Tangier in 1684 (see no. 16).

Within living memory, the Jews' River was a popular spot for washing clothes. Its remoteness, however, has more recently been surrendered to the Corniche (Route de la Plage Merkala), the modern coastal road that forges its way westwards from the Ferry Terminal to connect with the Route de la Vieille Montagne. Its construction saw much of the river culverted and parts of Merkala Beach paved over. Also lost was Merri's café. Little more than a shack built against the hillside without planning permission, it consisted of a terrace, a raised area for musicians and card players, and a long room with a bench, where customers could sit and watch the sea. The proprietor bolstered his income smuggling hashish out of Tangier on departing boats. It was most likely Merri's that Bowles was headed to on that clear day in 1987.

Another character associated with Merkala is the Tangier storyteller Mohamed Mrabet (b. 1936). One of twelve children and illiterate, he honed his craft in the city's cafés, whilst also providing *kif* and sexual favours to an American couple who befriended him.

Merkala Beach looking towards the Old Mountain

They took him to America but when the friendship soured, he returned to Tangier. Back home his propensity for violence got the better of him and he only evaded the law by hiding in a cave out beyond Merkala, where he survived on shrimps. Forgoing alcohol, in 1964 he encountered Paul Bowles (1910–1999) and his wife Jane (1917–1973) on Merkala Beach. Intrigued by Mrabet's stories, they offered to record, translate, and publish them as they had done a couple of years earlier with another local storyteller, Larbi Layachi (1937–1986), who worked at Merri's as a watchman. The result was the *kif*-fuelled *Love with a Few Hairs* (1967), a novel about love, betrayal, and sorcery in 1960s Tangier.

What remains of Merkala Beach is a stretch of sand backed by a seawall built of boulders. Youngsters still come here to swim and a rocky coastal path beyond is popular with fishermen. Beach lovers can head farther west to Achakkar, where a string of Atlantic beaches flank the Caves of Hercules (see no. 45). For Mediterranean beaches, head east to Malabata and Sidi Kankouch (see no. 52).

Other locations nearby: 35, 40, 41

40 Expats on the Old Mountain

Outer Suburbs: Old Mountain, a walk taking in some expatriate properties starting with the former home of Rupert Croft-Cooke on Imouzzar Avenue (note: most of the properties mentioned are private and closed to the public)

West of the Marshan stands the Old Mountain. This residential neighbourhood, with its cool north-facing aspect and sylvan setting, is home to some of Tangier's most attractive private properties. The King of Morocco and various Middle Eastern potentates keep second homes here, which explains the guards outside several gates. The neighbourhood's golden age, however, was really the 20th century, when 'the Mountain' attracted various well-to-do expatriate writers, artists, and eccentrics.

The Mountain is best reached by taxi or else bus number 4, which departs from Rue Sidi Bouabid, just west of the Grand Socco. After half a dozen stops, alight at the roundabout at Dradeb. From here the main road strikes north to Merkala Beach. Take the first left along Avenue Banafsaj and then bear right onto Rue Azrou at the red-domed building. The next right is Rue Sidi Masmoudi (known previously as Route de la Vieille Montagne), which snakes up the Mountain.

Far from the cramped conditions of the Medina, it is no surprise that expatriates were drawn here in search of freedom, friendship, and country pursuits (see no. 44). The first property of note, at the junction with the first street on the left (Imouzzar Avenue), is the most modest. "Four square and essentially Spanish" the now shabby concrete house dates from the early-1950s and was once home to the prolific but largely forgotten English author Rupert Croft-Cooke (1903–1979). His book *The Tangerine House* (1956) details the construction and furnishing of the house. Croft-Cooke penned more than 30 novels, just as many detective novels penned under the pseudonym Leo Bruce, 27 volumes of autobiography, and many works of non-fiction on topics as diverse as Buffalo Bill, sherry, darts, and Greek cooking!

Continuing up Rue Sidi Masmoudi past walled private gardens bursting with bougainvillea and mimosa, one reaches a sharp left turn. The eyecatching stuccoed gate here once led to an expatriate estate called Mount Washington since it was home to several early US consuls. Farther uphill, at another bend in the road, is a whitewashed property, with a distinctive tower, called El Foolk (The

Ark). This was originally owned by the artist Helen Russell Wilson (1872–1924) and then by the charismatic Scottish artist James McBey (1883–1959) and his wife, the American heiress Marguerite McBey née Loeb (1905–1999). The property was later acquired by British antiques dealer Christopher Gibbs (1938–2018). His partner, Peter Hinwood (b. 1946), who played Rocky in *The Rocky Horror Picture Show* (1975), occupied a cottage in the grounds.

The Mount Washington gate on the Old Mountain

At the next sharp turn but entirely concealed from the road is a property called Gazebo, which belongs to the New Zealand-born interior designer Veere Grenney (b. 1949). In 2009, he took a 1930s-era cottage occupied by writer Alan Sillitoe (1928–2010) during the early-1960s and transformed it into a magnificent modern villa, with cascading terraced gardens.

A little further on again a palm-lined drive on the left leads to the elegant Villa Joséphine. Built in the early-1920s by the renowned *Times* correspondent Walter Burton Harris (1866–1933), this magnificent property was later acquired by the Spanish aristocrat Ignacio de Figueroa y Bermejillo (1892–1953), 2nd Duke of Tovar (see no. 50). It then became the summer residence of Thami el Glaoui (1879–1956), Pasha of Marrakesh and Berber chieftain of the Glaoui tribe. Following Moroccan independence, the tribe forfeited its assets for having

El Foolk was once home to Scottish artist James McBey and his wife

conspired with the French to overthrow Sultan Mohammed V (1909–1961). Nowadays the villa is a luxurious 11-room hotel although less affluent visitors are welcome to take mint tea on the terrace.

Continuing along Rue Sidi Masmoudi, past a Muslim cemetery with its rows of Mecca-facing Islamic tombs, one reaches a fork in the road. Turn right here to reach the Villa Jalobey at number 312. This also once belonged to the McBeys, the villa's name being an amalgam of their names: James, Loeb and McBey. The property now belongs to the family of French-Moroccan artist Yto Barrada (b. 1971), who has created the Mothership, a natural dye garden, workshop, and artists' retreat here (open by appointment only).

Double back now, passing a hamlet on the left, where a track leads to the so-called Cherifian Rocks and the lonely grave of James McBey. Named for the Sherif of Ouezzane, Sidi Abdeslam (1834–1892), who once owned the land, the area now belongs to the American School of Tangier and can be visited on request.

Other locations nearby: 39, 41

41 Through a Moroccan Lens

Outer Suburbs: Old Mountain, the Fondation pour la Photographie Tanger at 235 Rue Sidi Masmoudi

On the Old Mountain there is a treat for photographers. The Fondation pour la Photographie Tanger is Morocco's first private endeavour dedicated to the promotion of contemporary photography. Located at 235 Rue Sidi Masmoudi, it was established in 2018 by Daniel and Françoise Aron.

Old photos at the Fondation pour la Photographie Tanger

Sharing his time between Paris and Tangier, Daniel Aron is well-versed in the art of photography. For many years, it was his photographs that helped reshape the public image of the French luxury brand Hermès, while he also collected awards for his advertising work in New York, Paris, Hamburg, and Milan. His images have graced the pages of some of the world's best-known glossy magazines, including *Harper's Bazaar* and *Vogue* (US), *Elle* and *Architectural Digest* (France), *Donna* (Germany), and *Hanatsubaki* (Japan). He has also staged photographic exhibitions in France and Morocco. In Tangier the venues have included the Kasbah Museum, French Institute, Instituto Cervantes, and Les Insolites bookshop

The permanent venue for the Fondation pour la Photographie Tanger is a bespoke minimalist structure of whitewashed concrete. Concealed from the road by forest, it consists of six exhibition spaces spread over two levels, a film laboratory, and a library dedicated to the visual arts. The mission is to promote photography as an art form through annual exhibitions and events, where the public can encounter both photographs and photographers, and vice versa. Exhibitions so far have included Aron's own black-and-white portraits of well-known cultural figures, images of Hollywood's anonymous from the collection of Robert Flynn Johnson, colourised photos from the period 1860–2022, and an exhibition on role-playing games featuring the work of female Moroccans such as Amina Benbouchta (b. 1963), Safaa Mazirh (b. 1989), and Fatima Zohra Serri (b. 1995).

Other locations nearby: 39, 40

42 The Perdicaris Affair

Outer Suburbs: Rmilat, the Villa Perdicaris in Rmilat Park

The past decade has seen a great revival in the fortunes of Tangier. In 2013, King Mohammed VI (b. 1963) launched his Tangier Metropolis and Tangier City Port redevelopment projects to bring Tangier into the 21st century. Along the way various historic properties have been renovated and opened to the public. One of these is the Villa Perdicaris in Rmilat, where just over a century ago a kidnapping brought American gunboats to the shores of Morocco.

The Perdicaris Villa was built by the American lawyer and artist Ion Hanford Perdicaris (1840–1925). Born in Athens, where his father was the first American Consul to Greece, Perdicaris grew up in the United States. There he became an international correspondent for *The Galaxy* magazine, subsequently absorbed into *The Atlantic* magazine. During a business trip to London, he was befriended by a retired French naval officer, who owned property in Morocco and invited Perdicaris to visit. Immediately charmed by the place, Perdicaris sought a base of his own there.

In 1872, he acquired a remote plot of land in the Rmilat Forest, five miles west of the Medina. Known as the Place of Nightingales, it was there that he built a whitewashed, turreted home he called Aidonia, with a verandah overlooking the sea. Once settled he became active in the international community and as a human rights activist and member of the anti-slave movement, set about fighting for the rights of the local people.

In 1904, Aidonia (today the Villa Perdicaris) made headline news. On the night of 18th May, it was raided by Mulai Ahmed er Raisuni (1871–1925), the leader of the Western Rif Jebala tribal confederacy. Considered a heroic figure by his followers for opposing Morocco's increasing subservience to foreign powers, Raisuli (as English speakers know him) was little more than a cattle-rustling brigand in the eyes of Sultan Abd al-Aziz (1878/1881–1943). Whatever the truth, he kidnapped Perdicaris and held him to ransom as he had the British journalist Walter Burton Harris (1866–1933) a year earlier (see no. 50).

News of the abduction soon reached the ears of American President Theodore Roosevelt (1858–1919). Running for a second term, he saw an opportunity to attract voter support by securing the safe return of an American citizen abroad. Accordingly, he issued the headline-friendly slogan "Perdicaris Alive or Raisuli Dead!" and

The Perdicaris Villa in Rmilat Park

ordered the South Atlantic Squadron of the United States Navy to Morocco. The Moroccan government, keen to preserve its long-standing good relations with the United States, acceded to Raisuli's demands. Perdicaris and his stepson were released and in return Raisuli received not only a large ransom but also the governorship of the Tangier and Jebala provinces. The episode is recounted in the heavily fictionalised film *The Wind and the Lion* (1975) starring Sean Connery as Raisuli.

Roosevelt's display of strength helped earn him a second presidential term but Raisuli was less fortunate. Falling in and out of favour with the Moroccan government and foreigners alike, he was eventually captured and imprisoned by fellow Riffian warlord Abd el-Krim (1882–1963). He died in his cell of dropsy several years later.

In 1910, Perdicaris left Morocco for England and retirement. Later, in 1930, his successors sold the villa to Thami el Glaoui (1879–1956), Pasha of Marrakesh, who occupied it when visiting Tangier. With Moroccan independence in 1956, the villa and its surrounding 70 hectares (173 acres) of forest became a state-owned park. Following a period of neglect, in 2015 the villa was restored and now serves as a centre for the interpretation of the park's natural heritage.

Other locations nearby: 43

43 A Garden by the Sea

Outer Suburbs: Rmilat, the Donabo Botanical Gardens on Route du Cap Spartel

Visitors to Tangier might not associate the place with gardens. In fact, the once-shabby port city is today surprisingly verdant. Its myriad green spaces include not only trim public parks and tree-lined roads tended by an army of municipal gardeners but also intimate domestic courtyards and flower-filled oases created by expats. There is also the Donabo Botanical Gardens, the first botanical garden in Tangier.

Located on Cape Spartel, the gardens are part of a sloping pine forest conservation area overlooking the Atlantic. It is the product of collaboration between Charifa Lalla Malika El Alaoui, whose father was a royal prince with long-standing connections to the area, and English decorative artist Paul Belvoir (b. 1963). Together they have created a magical woodland garden here.

The name 'Donabo' comes from the Latin *donare*, meaning 'to give'. It reflects not only the generosity of the fertile land with its natural springs and cool sea breezes but also the warm welcome accorded travellers visiting this part of the world. Donabo comprises ten distinct and clearly-marked pocket gardens laid out across a hectare (2.47 acres) of land. They radiate out from a scene-setting floral roundabout immediately beyond the ticket office, lined with banks of rosemary, sage, and thyme, overhung with lemon trees.

A sea view at the Donabo Botanical Gardens

The first garden, on the right, is a contemplative Chinese garden accessed through a circular Moon Gate. It is centred on a tranquil lily pond beneath bamboo and papyrus fronds. Beyond is a Moroccan garden, containing a wide variety of medicinal and culinary herbs. They include Oregano *(origanum vulgare)*, Wormwood *(artemisia absinthium)*, Winter Savory *(satureja montana)*, Fringed Rue *(ruta chalepensis)*, Turmeric *(curcuma longa)*, and Lemon Verbena *(aloysia citrodora)*.

Back on the main path is the Mint Maze, which contains more than twenty varieties of the plant that is a quintessential part of Moroccan culture and cuisine. Its Arabic name *nana* appears in mosaic on the garden's threshold. Spearmint *(mentha spicata)* is the main ingredient of mint tea (atay bin-nana), Morocco's national beverage since the mid-19th century, when British merchants introduced Chinese Gunpowder green tea to which Moroccans added mint leaves and sugar. Other mints on display include Apple Mint *(menthe suaveolens)*, Horse Mint *(mentha longifolia)*, Peppermint *(mentha piperita)*, Water Mint *(mentha aquatica)*, and the rare Atlas Mountain mint *(mentha suaveolens subsp. timija)*.

Next is a formal kitchen potager, which consists of a series of raised beds used for growing salad vegetables, including tomatoes, chard, courgettes, and fennel. Entirely organic, the produce is used in the adjacent cooking school. A separate space is used for growing chilli peppers, including Spanish Pepper *(capsicum annuum)*, Wild Chilli *(capsicum frutescens)*, and Habanero Pepper *(capsicum chinense)*.

The ten gardens are filled out with a trellised English rose garden, a pollination garden, where arching stems of *gaura* attract bees, butterflies, and other winged insects, a shady promenade, a hibiscus garden, and a rock garden. At the far end of the garden is a delightful café, which serves a fully organic menu. The views from the terrace out across the Strait of Gibraltar are sublime.

For visitors with a serious botanical interest, the garden's website details the 300-plus species grown on the site (www.donabogardens.com).

A remarkable private garden on Tangier's Atlantic coast is that of Italian horticulturalist and writer Umberto Pasti (b. 1957). Close to the village of Rohuna, it features a wildly romantic mix of olive and almond trees, damask roses, Madonna lilies, hollyhocks, and the rare Tangerian purple wild iris *(Iris Tingitana)*. Visits can be arranged at www.gardenofrohuna.com. To experience vicariously Pasti's achievements read his books *Eden Revisited: A Garden in Northern Morocco* (2019) and *The House of a Lifetime: A Collector's Journey in Tangier* (2023).

Other locations nearby: 42

44 The British Pet Cemetery

Outer Suburbs: New Mountain (California), the Animal Rest Home on Route de Boubana north of the Royal Country Club de Tanger (note: accessible all hours and easily visited by taxi on the way to Cape Spartel and the Caves of Hercules)

Tangier's British community has left various marks on the city. During the 20th century they built their own Anglican church (St. Andrew's) and frequented their favourite hotel (the El Minzah built by the wealthy Marquess of Bute) (see nos. 9, 21). Perhaps most typical is the cemetery they created for their beloved pets!

The origin of the cemetery is unclear. Some state that it dates back as far as the early-20th century, a claim supported by the headstone of one Danton seemingly dated 1902. Others reject this in favour of the early 1940s (Ginger's grave is dated 1943), when they say an unnamed British diplomat campaigned to improve the lot of the city's many beasts of burden forced to carry heavy loads to and from the souks. This zoophilist act prompted a British lady to acquire a plot of empty land on the New Mountain, a southern extension of the Old Mountain so popular with Tangier's well-to-do expatriates. There, in a bend in the so-called Jews' River, in a neighbourhood called California, she established a burial ground known as the Animal Rest Home, where deceased pets could be given a very British send-off and a headstone to boot. Africa's first animal cemetery, its preponderance of buried dogs explains why on some maps it is marked as the *Cimetière Canin*.

During the 1950s, the cemetery was championed by resident British socialite and writer David Herbert (1908–1995), as well as the celebrated American writer Paul Bowles (1910–1999). The latter went so far as to declare that "If I have to be buried in the ground, I'd like it to be in the animal cemetery here in Tangier, along with the dogs and cats that belonged to the European residents … I do rather relish the thought of lying anonymously amidst the Fidos and Rexes and aged eucalyptus trees that shade their graves". When it came to it, Bowles was buried in upstate New York.

Since the end of the Tangier International Zone in 1956, the cemetery has slowly been given over to Mother Nature. Although new graves are still dug, many of the old ones are toppled and broken. Those still intact include "unforgettable" Kira (d. 1964), "compagnon fidèle" Hugo (d. 1970), and "little shining star" Pooki (d. 2022).

The cemetery is surrounded by several other British relics. To the east, for example, is the Royal Equestrian Club, whilst immediately south lies the Royal Country Club of Tangier. It was here in 1914 that Sultan Abd al-Aziz (1878/1881–1943) established Morocco's first golf course, which offered nine holes to eager British golfers. Before that, the Tangier Tent Club was here, on land that formed part of the so-called Diplomatic Forest, where British diplomats were granted the right to pursue the grisly sport of pig-sticking.

The author examines a headstone at the Animal Rest Home

Visitors who enjoy burial grounds might like to know that just north of the animal cemetery is the Boubana Christian Cemetery. Administered by foreigners during the time of the Tangier International Zone (1925–1956), it is here that French, Spanish, Italian, and Belgian Catholics, who emigrated to Tangier to work, are buried in Moorish-style box tombs adorned with bunches of gladioli and calla lilies. Farther south, beyond the golf course and straddling the Route Mojahidine, is the Mojahidine Cemetery, one of the largest in Tangier, with thousands of Muslim graves facing east towards Mecca.

Regarding beasts of burden, Tangier is unique in laying claim to a dedicated Donkey Museum. Located at 49 Rue de la Kasbah (Marshan), the two-room premises celebrate the animal's importance in Moroccan life through art, literature, and public events.

45 The Caves of Hercules

Outer Suburbs: Achakkar, the Caves of Hercules at the end of Route des Grottes d'Hercule

Tangier is steeped in myth and legend. According to Classical mythology, the city gets its name from Tinge, the daughter of Atlas and wife of the giant Antaeus. Hercules, son of Zeus, battled and defeated Antaeus, whilst travelling to the Garden of the Hesperides to steal the golden apples as part of his Twelve Labours. Hercules then fathered a son with Tinge called Sophax, who founded Tangier and named it in honour of his mother.

In Greek legend, Heracles (as they know Hercules) offers to support the heavens on his shoulders whilst Atlas retrieves the golden apples for him. Atlas then attempts to trick Heracles into carrying the heavens permanently but the ruse fails leaving Heracles to escape with the apples. Roman sources have Hercules crossing a chain of mountains connecting Europe to Africa to reach the Garden of the Hesperides. Instead of climbing the mountains, Hercules uses his superhuman strength to smash through them. In doing so, he connects the Atlantic Ocean to the Mediterranean Sea forming the Strait of Gibraltar in the process (geologists know this event as the Zanclean Flood, which they theorize may have happened 5.3 million years ago). The rocks remaining on either side of the Strait have since been known as the Pillars of Hercules. After such exertions, Hercules is then said to have rested in a set of sea caves. These same caves can be visited today in the suburb of Achakkar, nine miles south-west of Tangier.

Legend aside, the Caves of Hercules are no ordinary caves. Part natural and part manmade, they have two openings, one landwards and one out to sea. The natural part was created by the action of waves crashing through a portal shaped coincidentally like the continent of Africa. The manmade part was the work of the Berbers, who entered through a land portal to extract material for millstones, leaving the curious half-moon cuts that can be seen inside the caves and on the rocks on the shoreline below. Archaeological evidence suggests that Neolithic people sheltered here around 8,000 BC, as did the Phoenicians and Romans later.

The caves were first opened to the public in 1920, although electric lighting was not installed until 1982. Photographer and costumier Cecil Beaton (1904–1980) hosted a party in the caves in 1949 with hashish and sea-cooled Champagne for the guests. In 1987, the ashes of the artist and inventor Brion Gysin (1916–1986), were sprinkled above the cave, and in 1995 the British rock group Def Leppard played a concert here as part of their successful bid to play three concerts on three continents in one day. A tall story pertaining to the cave is that it was once the entrance to a tunnel used by Barbary apes to travel under the sea to Gibraltar!

The Africa-shaped sea portal at the Caves of Hercules

The Caves of Hercules today have become a popular visitor attraction and have attracted all the usual accoutrements of such places. Accordingly, there is a plaza outside the cave entrance with gift shops, restaurants, and cafés. Access to the caves is down a ramp in one corner of the plaza. Be aware that just before the entrance there is a separate landlocked cave that contains rather kitsch life-sized models of Hercules undertaking his labours, an artificial waterfall, a gift shop, and locals offering photo opportunities with various chained birds and monkeys.

A short way back along the main road to Tangier is another less famous cave. The Grotte des Chevaux is a natural cave system that sits above a stretch of water.

Other locations nearby: 46

46 The Cape Spartel Lighthouse

Outer Suburbs: Achakkar, the Cape Spartel Lighthouse on Route Agla (note: wild boars inhabit the nearby forest and if seen should not be approached)

Seven and a half miles south-west of Tangier is Cape Spartel. This pine-covered headland is the northwesternmost point of Africa and can be reached by taking the National Road S701 from Tangier over the Jebel Kebir (Big Mountain). Perched on a cliff at the end of Route Agla, a thousand feet above the spectacular rocky seashore, is the Cape Spartel lighthouse (see front cover).

Marking the entrance to the Strait of Gibraltar and completed in 1864, the lighthouse was commissioned by Sultan Mohammed IV (1803–1873). A year later, in one of the first examples of international co-operation in Tangier, the Spartel Lighthouse Treaty was signed by the Sultan, the Moroccan Government, and ten foreign powers, including the French, Spanish, and Americans. It only returned to full Moroccan control after the country gained full independence in 1956.

The lighthouse consists of a 79-foot-high, square masonry tower reminiscent of a minaret. It supports an elegant lantern containing a 20,000-candle power composite Fresnel lens. From the crenellated balcony at the top, which is reached by a magnificent cantilevered spiral stone staircase, some expansive seascapes are to be had.

Attached to the base of the lighthouse is a courtyard that contained the lighthouse keepers' accommodation and stores. In several of the rooms a maritime museum has been set up giving technical specifications of the light, images of the various lighthouse keepers down through the ages, and details of the naval engagements and sinkings that have occurred off the cape. These include the destruction of six Barbary Pirate vessels by the English and Dutch navies in August 1670, the capture of two Spanish gunships by the British in 1704, and an inconclusive battle between British and Franco-Spanish vessels in 1782. In 1911, the British P&O liner *SS Delhi* ran aground off Cape Spartel but fortunately all 243 passengers were rescued.

On the windswept seaward terrace, a signpost lays claim to being the spot where the Atlantic Ocean meets the Mediterranean Sea (although a popular parking spot a little further south makes the same claim). There is also a modern decorative iron sculpture, the so-called Sunset Catcher, through the centre of which the sun can be seen to set between June and August.

Where the Atlantic meets the Mediterranean at Cape Spartel

A complete renovation of the lighthouse and its immediate surroundings was completed in 2021. As a result, today's visitors can enjoy not only the lighthouse but also some surprisingly lush gardens and a restaurant. Don't miss the larger-than-life portrait of the current king in dark suit and sunglasses!

The Cape Spartel headland is also a nature reserve popular with ornithologists. They come here in late-March to early-April to watch birds migrating to Europe, and again in October to watch them as they return. Species include black kites *(Milvus migrans)*, booted eagles *(Hieraaetus pennatus)*, and white storks *(Ciconia ciconia)*.

Just offshore from the lighthouse is Spartel Bank, a sunken island that vanished around 12,000 years ago. Some commentators have equated it with the lost island of Atlantis. This is hardly surprising considering that the ancient Greek philosopher Plato placed the legendary city "beyond the Pillars of Hercules", in other words in the Atlantic beyond the two rocky promontories that flank the entrance to the Strait of Gibraltar. The northern pillar is the Rock of Gibraltar. The corresponding southern pillar is the subject of discussion but is most likely Jebel Musa in Morocco or Monte Hacho in the Spanish autonomous city of Ceuta.

Other locations nearby: 45

47 The Gift of Sport

Outer Suburbs: Ziaten, the Cité des Sports (Sports Village) between Avenue Moulay Rachid and the N1 highway

The accession of King Mohammed VI (b. 1963) to the throne of Morocco has been good for Tangier. Unlike his father, Hassan II (1929–1999), who distrusted Tangier for its association with foreigners, the new king has invested heavily in the city's infrastructure, including a new port, high-speed rail link, and Africa's largest carbon-neutral car factory. Especially popular with the city's younger generation is the Cité des Sports, a world-class sporting complex in the southern suburb of Ziaten.

The Cité des Sports, or Sports Village as Tanjawis call it, is part of the king's ambitious Tangier Metropolis urban regeneration project. It occupies an enormous site covering 74 hectares (182 acres) between Avenue Moulay Rachid and the N1 highway. Completed in 2021 at a cost of one billion Moroccan Dirhams (£82 million), it received support from various state ministries, the Urban Municipality of Tangier, and the private sector. Thus far it has fulfilled admirably its main objectives: to create a focal point for the city's enthusiastic sports'

The Ibn Battouta Stadium will be used for the 2030 FIFA World Cup

community; to bring together outdoor and indoor sports amenities on a single site; and to give Tangier the means to host major sporting events and to be taken seriously at an international level. Perhaps most importantly, the Cité des Sports is providing the young people of Tangier with an outlet for their sporting energies and hopefully producing a few world champions along the way.

As Africa's most comprehensive collection of state-of-the-art sporting facilities, the complex comprises ten main elements. First and foremost is the enormous oval-shaped Ibn Battouta Football Stadium named in honour of the city's famous son and currently the largest structure in Tangier (see no. 14). Located in the centre of the site, with seating for 65,000 spectators, including provision for 500 VIP guests, the stadium is used for official championship and cup matches. It also includes a media centre and an infirmary, The stadium was inaugurated in 2011, as part of a tournament that included the prominent local professional team Ittihad Riada Tanger. It is currently being revamped in preparation for the 2030 FIFA World Cup, when Morocco, Spain and Portugal will co-host the event.

Ranged around the stadium are various smaller facilities. To the east is a covered football pitch, an athletics track, a 4,000-seat football stadium used by amateur clubs in the Northern League, and the training ground of Ittihad Riada Tanger (after all this is their home ground). To the west is an indoor, 3,500-seat tennis stadium, with 17 outdoor training courts attached, the large multipurpose Arena Olympic Hall, and two small indoor halls, one for mini-football *(futsal)* and another for the popular French game of *pétanque*. Also in this part of the complex is the Olympic Swimming Pool (Piscine Olympique), with space for 2,000 spectators. There is also a separate pool for young swimmers.

The facilities are rounded out to the north with a couple more open-air football pitches and a covered hall (Salle Omnisports de Tanger), which acts as an entrance to the complex for visitors approaching from the Avenue Moulay Rachid. Like the Arena Olympic Hall, it is a multidisciplinary space that can be used for a variety of team sports, including basketball, volleyball, and handball. Elsewhere on the site there are two hotels, a sports clinic, and a shopping mall selling sports equipment.

Half way between the stadium and the airport stands the Bab al-Andalous Mosque (on the right as one approaches the airport). An architectural masterpiece, it is one of the most beautiful of Tangier's many mosques.

48 A Spanish Bullring

Ville Nouvelle (New City), the former Plaza de Toros at the junction of Avenue Yacoub El Mansour and the N2 Route de Tétouan

Between 1925 and 1956, the victors of the Great War administered Tangier as an International Zone. Each left a mark on the city's architectural landscape in the form of banks, post offices, embassies, and churches. Perhaps the most distinctive legacy was that left by the Spanish, who not only built their own theatre but also a bullring.

Located at the junction of Avenue Yacoub El Mansour and the N2 Route de Tétouan, the bullring (Plaza de Toros), which opened in 1950, was established by two local businessmen, Jalid Raisuni and José Beneish. They engaged the engineer Francisco Rodrigálvarez López to design the huge circular structure, which had seating for just over 13,000 people. It also contained pens for the bulls and stables for the horses, as well as dressing rooms for the *matadors* (*toreros* in Spanish). There was a chapel, too, where *matadors* prayed before bouts, as well as veterinary facilities and a clinic in the event of injury.

At that time, most bullfighters were indeed *matadors*, including local heroes Pepito Medina, Jesús Cañizares, Primo Díaz y Campos, and Manolo Bernal. There was, however, at least one *matadora*, namely Conchita Cintrón (1922–2009), known as *La Diosa de Oro*

Tangier's old Spanish bullring is now a cultural centre

(The Golden Goddess). Born Concepción Cintrón Verrill in Chile, she fought in Tangier at a time when women were still prohibited from bullfighting in Spain.

The layout of the bullring followed that of Roman amphitheatres, where spectator blood sports originated. The audience sat in tiered stalls known as *tendidos*. The matador entered the sand-covered arena through one gate, while the bull was released through another. The audience was protected by a barrier, with wooden shields *(burladeros)* attached ringside for the protection of the matadors. The bullfight itself, known as a *corrida*, consisted of three stages or *tercios*. In the first, the flamboyantly-dressed matador assessed the intelligence and speed of the bull by taunting it with his (or her) red cape *(capote)*. Assistants *(peones)* then drew the bull away towards horsemen *(picadores)*, whose job it was to weaken the animal's neck muscles using steel-tipped lances *(varas)*. During the second stage, the wounded bull was weakened further by the matador sticking darts *(bandilleras)* in its back. During the third and final stage, the matador made a series of graceful passes at the bull with a smaller cape on a wooden pole *(muleta)*. Picking his moment, he dispatched the bull as cleanly and quickly as possible with a long thin sword.

The bullring in Tangier had a mercifully short life and closed in 1956, the year of Moroccan independence. Thereafter it was used for various sporting and cultural events, and during the last two decades of the 20th century it served as a detention center for sub-Saharan immigrants. Declared a National Historic Monument of Morocco in 2016, the former bullring is currently in the throes of being converted into a cultural centre containing an open-air space for art exhibitions, a covered exhibition hall, a 7,000-seat theatre, restaurants, and shops.

The bullring has as its backdrop a hill called the Charf. Partly covered in housing, the rest is taken up with a sprawling Muslim cemetery. According to local legend, the Charf was the burial place of the mythological giant Antaeus after his defeat by Hercules (see no. 45). The panoramic view from the top takes in all Tangier from Cape Malabata in the east across to the Old Mountain in the west. The needle-like minaret of the Syrian Mosque was built by a wealthy Syrian expatriate family, one of many who fled the upheaval of the Ba'ath Party takeover of their homeland in 1963.

Other locations nearby: 49

49 High Speed from Casablanca

Outer Suburbs: Malabata, Tanger Ville Railway Station (Gare Tanger Ville) at the junction of Avenue d'Espagne and Avenue de France

The Avenue Mohammed VI hugs the coastline of Tangier all the way from the ferry terminal beneath the Medina eastwards to Malabata. Its naming is a testament to the vision of Morocco's current king (b. 1963), who has done much to re-invent the city's waterfront. Part way along, between the junctions with Rue de la Plage and Rue du Portugal, there is a long, low building, with three doorways surmounted by an ornate grille and clock. Built in 1925, this was once Tangier's main railway station, delivering passengers and freight directly to and from the Old Port. It was serviced by the 196-mile-long Tangier–Fez railway. Traversing French- and Spanish-administered Morocco, as well as the Tangier International Zone (1925–1956) the line was constructed by a Franco-Spanish company and completed in 1927. It was here at the old railway station during the early-1940s that the Moroccan storyteller Mohamed Choukri (1935–2003) loitered when he first arrived in Tangier from Tétouan, his family having been forced out of their Rif Mountain home by drought.

Following the station's closure in 2003, when the port was relocated and the track bed lifted to make way for the Avenue Mohammed VI, it became a government building and later a police station. Today, it is home to the Port de Tanger Ville Société de Gestion, the body responsible for ferry and pleasure boat infrastructure in the new Tanja Bay Marina.

The replacement station, located where Avenue d'Espagne joins Avenue de France (Malabata), is further evidence of the king's vision (see no. 27). Opened the same year as the old station closed, it is administered by Morocco's national rail operator, the Office National des Chemins de Fer (ONCF), which was formed in 1963 by merging the country's four existing railway companies.

Called Tanger Ville Railway Station (Gare Tanger Ville), it is an impressive steel and concrete structure conceived in a modern Moroccan style by the architect Youssef Melehi. The rectangular terminal building has a tower at each corner. These have vents at the top to aid cross ventilation, and panels of colourful *zellij* tiles for decoration. The terminal's roof is made of arches running in two directions so that natural light is admitted from all sides whilst also providing necessary shade (it is also covered with photovoltaic sensors to reduce energy consumption).

The Al-Boraq high speed train arrives from Casablanca

Inside the terminal there are three halls loosely inspired by traditional Moroccan urban spaces. Thus, the main concourse resembles a *souk*, with retail outlets around the perimeter; the departures hall has the air of a *caravanserai*; and the boarding area is conceived as a garden, which helps keep the station cool during the summer months. This is important since only 10% of the terminal building is air-conditioned.

Beyond the terminal building are seven tracks and five canopied platforms. As well as carrying trains departing for Fez and Marrakesh, one of the tracks is used by the 201-mile-long Al-Boraq service, Africa's first high-speed rail link, which connects Tangier with Rabat and Casablanca. Inaugurated in 2018, it reaches speeds of up to 200 miles per hour between Tangier and the city of Kenitra, arriving in Rabat in an hour and Casablanca in one hour and 40 minutes (it will soon be possible to reach Marrakesh in two hours and forty minutes). The name of the line, which means 'lightning' in Arabic, is a reference to the winged horse ridden by the prophet Mohammed (570–632) during his night journey from Mecca to Jerusalem *(Isra)* and his subsequent ascension into heaven *(Mi'raj)*. Having served three million passengers in 2019, the station will most likely handle double that figure by 2030.

Other locations nearby: 48, 50, 51

50 The Villa Harris

Outer Suburbs: Malabata, the Villa Harris Museum at the junction of Boulevard Mohammed VI and Route Hassania

Several historical characters have been put forward as the inspiration for the adventure hero Indiana Jones. One of them is the writer, traveller, and socialite, Walter Burton Harris (1866–1933), who for many years was a Tangier-based special correspondent for *The Times* of London. He achieved considerable fame through his daring journeys, diplomatic connections, and literary achievements. In the 1890s, he built an elegant villa in Moorish Revival style facing the beach at Malabata. In recent years it has been transformed into an excellent art gallery.

Born in London, the son of a successful shipping merchant, Harris had already travelled the world by age eighteen. In 1887, he accompanied a British diplomatic mission to Morocco and settled in Tangier. Independently wealthy and with a writing stipend from *The Times*, he set about exploring. With his mastery of French, Spanish, and Arabic, and the ability to pass himself off as a native, he travelled into the heart of the country, where few Europeans had been. The result was not only a much-praised book called *The Land of an African Sultan* (1889) but also the respect and confidence of many Moroccans, including several sultans and high-ranking politicians. His most unlikely friendship was with the Riffian tribal leader Raisuli (1871–1925), who in 1903 briefly held Harris to ransom (see no. 42).

In 1906, Harris was made a permanent correspondent for *The Times*. He had a ringside seat in the years running up to Morocco being made a joint French and Spanish Protectorate (1912), as well as Tangier becoming an International Zone in 1925. Some diplomats regarded Harris as a useful go-between thanks to his extensive local contacts, whereas others disliked him. For example, he initially opposed French ambitions and instead favoured Germany, only to be told that he was undermining British diplomatic actions and should support the French, whose administrative efforts he eventually came to admire. His fascinating book from the period *Morocco that Was* (1921) is still in print today.

In 1933, Harris succumbed to a stroke whilst on board a ship in the Mediterranean. His body was returned to Tangier and buried in the graveyard of the Anglican Church of St. Andrew (see no. 21). Thereafter, his villa at Malabata served as a casino and later a beach resort before being abandoned in 1992. The villa's elaborate *zellij* tilework, decorative stucco, and carved cedar wood were left to rot until 2007,

The restored Villa Harris is now an excellent art museum

when the building was declared to be of national historic value and subsequently restored to its former glory. In 2021 it reopened as an art museum encompassing two centuries of art in Morocco.

The Villa Harris Museum documents three periods in the development of Moroccan and Moroccan-themed art using works donated by the collector El Khalil Belguench, who believed that all Moroccans should have the chance to view such material. The first illustrates the fascination of travelling Western painters with the light, colour, and landscape of Morocco and includes works by Orientalists such as Eugene Delacroix (1798–1863), Jacques Majorelle (1886–1962), Edy Legrand (1892–1970), and Claudio Bravo (1936–2011). The second focusses on Moroccan artists who were influenced by Western modernists, including Mohammed Ben Ali R'bati (1861–1939), Ahmed Yacoubi (1928–1985), Mohammed Hamri (1932–2000), and Farid Belkahia (1934–2014). The third period covering the 1950s, 60s, and 70s illustrates the coming of age of contemporary Moroccan art that breaks the earlier constraints of Berber and Islamic art. It includes works by the likes of Jilali Gharbaoui (1930–1971), Ahmed Cherkaoui (1934–1967), and the influential 'Casablanca Group', which had at its core Farid Belkahia (1934–2014), Mohammed Chabaa (1935–2013) and Mohamed Melehi (1936–2020).

Other locations nearby: 49, 51

51 A New Palace of Culture

Outer Suburbs: Malabata, the Palace of Arts and Culture (Palais des Arts et Culture de Tanger) at the junction of Avenue Mohammed VI and Route Hassania

During the 1890s, the Moroccan explore, *The Times* correspondent, and Tanjawi socialite Walter Burton Harris (1866–1933) built an elegant villa facing the beach at Malabata (see no. 50). The Villa Harris is still there today but its remoteness has in recent times been lost to housing and hotels. One of these new-builds now blocks the villa's once far-reaching sea views. This is the Palace of Arts and Culture (Palais des Arts et Culture de Tanger) at the junction of Avenue Mohammed VI and Route Hassania.

Completed in 2020, the building certainly warrants its 'palatial' name tag. The bold coastal location and the price tag of nearly 210 million Moroccan Dirhams (£17 million) bear witness to the cultural and economic ambition of King Mohammed VI (b. 1963), who has expended vast resources on reviving Tangier's waterfront as part of his Tangier Metropolis urban regeneration project.

The main curving façade of the palace reflects traditional Moroccan architecture, with its arched and horseshoe-shaped windows, *Mashrabiya*-style latticed screens, and six red-tiled towers,

The impressive Palace of Arts and Culture at Malabata

with plantings of palm trees to complete the scene. Inside, the building boasts an impressive 260,000 square feet of floor space spread generously across a 1,400-seat main auditorium and two flanking 200-seat halls. Modern in its overall appearance, the interior also makes a nod to the past with its high-quality artisanal woodwork.

The palace aims to be a multidisciplinary facility, one that will reinforce Tangier's status as a leading cultural destination both nationally and internationally. On the one hand, it will host world class concerts and performances as was borne out in 2024, when the palace was the nominated concert venue for International Jazz Day. On the other, the palace contains all the facilities required to host educational workshops for local students, as well as conferences and other events. In addition to its three performance halls, the palace includes four pavilions dedicated to learning and artistic practice, two art galleries, meeting rooms, a recording studio, café, restaurant, and children's area.

The Palace of Arts and Villa Harris are separated from the rest of Tangier by a broad shallow river valley watered by the Wadi el-Halk. Currently unculverted, the river's multiple branches fan out across the area so far defying the encroachment of modern development. Indeed the only manmade structure of note currently is a ruined British redoubt built to deter Berber raids during the 17th century (see no. 16).

Many visitors will be unaware that Jazz has played a significant role in Tangier's musical scene. During the 20th century, several American Jazz musicians spent time in the city, including Josephine Baker (1906–1975), Archie Shepp (b. 1937), and Robert 'Juice' Wilson (1904–1993). Others were inspired to compose works about the place, for example Ornette Coleman (1930–2015) *(Interzone Suite)*, Herbie Mann (1930–2003) *(In Tangier)*, and Idrees Sulieman (1923–2002) *(Tangier Blues)*. Another was Randy Weston (1926–2018) *(Tangier Bay)*, who lived in Tangier during the 1960s and 70s. He advanced the widely accepted theory that Jazz is essentially African music and also opened the African Rhythms club in the city with Moroccan producer and radio presenter Jacques Muyal (b. 1941). Weston famously collaborated with *gnawa* musician Abdellah El Gourd (b. 1947) to create a unique fusion of Moroccan music and Jazz (see no. 7). Jazz is still popular in Tangier, with regular live performances at the Hotel Chellah at 47–49 Rue Allal Ben Abdellah (Ville Nouvelle), as well as concerts, festivals, and workshops.

Other locations nearby: 49, 50

52 Malabata and Beyond

Outer Suburbs: Malabata, a trip out to Cape Malabata and its lighthouse at the end of Sidi Mnari

If it is sea views one is after, then Cape Spartel to the west of Tangier is a must. The handsome lighthouse with its sea views and visitor amenities certainly draws the visitors (see no. 46). To escape the crowds, however, there is an alternative. Head eastwards along Avenue Mohammed VI to join the coast road, National Route 16. After five or six miles turn left along Sidi Mnari, at the far end of which one finds Cape Malabata (Arabic *Ras Malabata*) overlooking the Strait of Gibraltar.

The lighthouse at Cape Malabata sports the Moroccan emblem

Despite encroaching building, farming, and quarrying, Cape Malabata retains an air of wild abandonment. Still partially clad in forest, the main point of interest is a lighthouse built in 1924. Its façade carries the five-pointed green star of the Moroccan flag rendered in plaster (the five points represent the Five Pillars of Islam).

Admittedly there is little to do here except wander around beneath the windswept pine and eucalyptus trees, and perhaps enjoy a mint tea at one of the wayside cafés. The distant views of Tarifa on the southern coast of Spain, however, as well as back along the coast to Tangier are well worth the journey and at sunset and sunrise you may well have the place to yourself.

Returning along Sidi Mnari, note the eyecatching ruin with corner turrets on a hill on the left-hand side behind the Café Restaurant Castillo. Dirt tracks wind up to what is sometimes known as Château de Mnar (*mnar* being Arabic for 'lighthouse' hence 'minaret'). It has been claimed, incorrectly, that the castle is 400 years' old and the work of the Portuguese. In fact it is an unfinished mock-medieval restaurant built in the 1920s by an Italian entrepreneur.

It is worth mentioning here another as-yet unfulfilled project. In 1930, a tunnel beneath the Strait of Gibraltar was proposed to link Cape Malabata with Punta Paloma in Spain. Revived again recently, the current idea is to tether prefabricated concrete tunnels to the seabed as a means of avoiding damage through tectonic activity. Time will tell whether the enormously ambitious project will ever be realised.

A trip to Cape Malabata can be extended by continuing eastwards another 13 miles on the N16 to the former medieval town of Ksar es-Seghir. Its name means 'small castle' and as a military fort it saw activity from the Phoenician period onwards. Its sheltered position made it particularly useful as a transit point for seaborne troops. The ruined walls of the Portuguese-era fortifications, erected in 1502, overlook the mouth of a small river and run right down onto the beach. Adjacent to the ruins is the Restaurant Laachiri, which is famous for its fish and seafood platters. There are also several pristine sandy beaches in the area.

Returning to Tangier from Cape Malabata, the coastline is one continuous beach. Beach clubs have replaced the old bars so popular during the 20th century with the city's expatriate *demi-monde*. Joe Orton (1933–1967) and his lover Kenneth Halliwell (1926–1967), for example, drank at the Windmill, Rupert Croft-Cooke (1903–1979) frequented the Mar Chica, and Tennessee Williams (1911–1983) topped up his tan at the Sun Beach. The Moroccan storytellers Mohamed Mrabet (b. 1936) and Larbi Layachi (1937–1986) roamed the beach before their life-changing encounters with American author Paul Bowles (1910–1999). A century earlier, Alexandre Dumas (1802–1870) challenged a local tribesman to a shooting competition here and *The Times* journalist Walter Burton Harris (1866–1933) built a private villa here (see no. 50).

53 East to Tétouan

Farther Afield: Tétouan, a day trip to the former capital of the Spanish Moroccan Protectorate (note: Tétouan is easily accessible from Tangier by bus, train, or car)

The city of Tétouan is located 37 miles east of Tangier. One of Morocco's major Mediterranean ports, it sits on the northern slope of the fertile Martil River valley, overlooked by the brooding massifs of the western Rif mountains. A day trip is recommended not only for the city's UNESCO-listed Medina (Old City) but also its unique fusion of Spanish and Moroccan culture.

The story of Tétouan began during the 3rd century BC, when Mauretanian Berbers established a settlement a few miles west of the modern city limits. They were followed a century later by Phoenician traders and after them came the Romans, who established the Roman colony of Tamuda. Its modest ruins are still visible on the south side of the river.

Fast forward now to the late-13th century, when the Berber Marinid Dynasty (1244–1465) founded a Kasbah and mosque in what is today Tétouan's Medina. Expanded during the early-14th century, these were destroyed a century later by the Castilians in

A mosque and houses in the city of Tétouan

retaliation for piracy. Following the *Reconquista* of Spain by the Catholics in 1492, many Muslim and Jewish refugees relocated from Andalusia to northern Morocco, including Tétouan, which was rebuilt. It became known by the Muslims as 'Granada's Daughter' and by the Jews as 'Little Jerusalem'.

During the second half of the 17th century, the Alawi governor of Tangier took Tétouan. He commissioned the construction of the Royal Palace, the Grand Mosque, and the crenellated fortifications around the Medina. Much later, in 1913, Tétouan became the capital of the Spanish Protectorate of Morocco, which it remained until Moroccan independence in 1956. The influence of Spain continued into modern times, with Spanish still spoken in the city today, alongside the more usual French and Arabic, as well as a separate Tétouan dialect.

There is much to see in Tétouan. The Medina is one of the most authentic in all Morocco. Until the 20th century its seven gates were still locked at night and its public fountains were supplied by an underground water system built by Andalusian refugees. An easy walking tour commences at Feddan Park in the city centre, which affords a fine view of the city's walled Kasbah on a hill to the north. From here head west along Avenue Alger (*outside* the old walls) and take the first right. At the far end there are souks on either side. Turn right to enter the enormously atmospheric Souk El Fuuki, a linear covered market that stretches the length of Rue Laayoun to the Bab M'Kabar gate. Here can be found the city's abandoned 16th century tannery.

Directly south is the Royal Palace, which looks out onto Place el Mechouar. Opposite is the excellent Archaeological Museum with its Stone Age tools, Roman mosaics, and Andalusian-style garden containing a collection of Jewish, Muslim, and Christian grave stelae. The former Jewish quarter (*mellah*) lies south of the palace, beyond which is the Riad Al Ochak ('Lovers Garden') and the Tétouan Modern Art Centre.

If time permits, one should stray into the Ville Nouvelle (New City). During the time of Spanish administration, new rectilinear neighbourhoods were laid out here immediately west of the Medina. Known as *Ensanche* ('extension'), they feature whitewashed Art Deco and Rationalist façades like those found in other Spanish cities during the first half of the 20th century. These neighbourhoods radiate out from the large circular Plaza Moulay el-Mehdi, known originally as the Plaza Primo de Rivera.

54 South to Chefchaouen

Farther Afield: Chefchaouen, a day trip into the Rif Mountains (note: Chefchaouen is easily accessible from Tangier by bus or car)

Some sixty miles south of Tangier is the town of Chefchaouen. The name is of Arabic origin, being an amalgam of *chef* ('to look') and *chaouen* ('horns'). The full translation 'look at the horns' reflects the town's setting between two peaks in the foothills of the western Rif Mountains. Situated 2,000 feet above sea leavel, Chefchaouen provides not only a geographical change from Tangier but also an opportunity to witness the living culture of the Berber (more correctly Amazigh) people.

Ali ibn Rashid al-Alami (c. 1440–1512), leader of the mujahideen in north-west Morocco, founded Chefchaouen in 1471 as a fortress *(Kasbah)* from which to repel Portuguese incursions. After the 1492 *Reconquista*, when Spanish Christians conquered al-Andalus, many Muslims, Moriscos, and Jews relocated to the large cities of Morocco. Others, however, chose Chefchaouen, where they merged with the existing Ghomara people, who remain part of the Jebala federation of Berber tribes. The Medina (Old City), with its gates and mosques, was established outside the Kasbah at this time.

Chefchaouen's other significant brush with history came in 1920, when Spanish forces occupied the city and it became a part of the Spanish Protectorate in Morocco. Between 1924 and 1926, it was briefly retrieved by Abd el-Krim (c. 1882–1963) to form part of his Republic of the Rif. Quickly retaken by the Spanish Army, it then remained under Spanish administration until Moroccan independence in 1956.

As with other Moroccan towns and cities, most visitors head straight for the Medina. The traditional houses here consist of rooms ranged around an open courtyard often planted with fruit trees and jasmine in the Andalusian style. At the heart of the Medina is Place Outa el-Hammam (named after the public bathhouse here), which contains the Great Mosque and a 16th century caravanserai *(fondouk)* with a horseshoe-shaped entrance built to house visiting merchants. In the centre of the square is a traditional fountain *(saqiyah)* and there are shops, where traditional Moroccan handicrafts, notably leather goods, wooden items, and textiles, can be bought. The ankle-length hooded garment known as a *djellaba* is said to have originated in Chefchaouen.

The Kasbah is protected by its own set of walls made from rammed earth punctuated by ten towers of the same construction. Inside there is a tranquil Andalusian-style courtyard garden and a 17th century house containing an archaeological and ethnographic museum. The southernmost neighbourghood of the Medina is called Souika after the first souk established there in the 15th century. A Jewish neighbourhood or *mellah* followed later.

The famous blue-painted walls of Chefchaouen

It is interesting to note that some local families have preserved the art of Andalusian music, which remains a feature of the religious and secular festivals they still observe. It can be heard, for example, on days when they visit the shrines *(zawiya)* of local holy men.

Outside the east wall of the Medina is a rushing mountain stream, the Ras al-Ma' (literally 'water head'), which is lined with cafés and fruit stalls popular with visiting locals. On the hill above is a disused mosque built by the Spanish in the 1920s, which provides a view over the town and surrounding Rif Mountains.

In recent decades, Chefchaouen has been marketed as the Blue Pearl of Morocco for its photogenic indigo-coloured lime-washed houses. It is said that the choice of blue was to deter mosquitoes or to act as a reminder that people should work towards heaven. A more cynical explanation is that the walls were painted this way simply to attract tourists. Whatever the truth, they are enormously photogenic.

55 West to Asilah

Farther Afield: Asilah, a day trip to the Atlantic coast (note: Asilah is easily accessible from Tangier by bus, train, or car)

Barely 20 miles south-west of Tangier is the coastal town of Asilah. Its well-preserved fortifications, spruced-up Medina, and sandy beach make for a good day out for those wishing to escape the bustle and urban sprawl of Tangier.

The history of Asilah broadly mirrors that of Tangier. It was founded as the port of Silis (sometimes Zilis) by the Phoenicians as early as 1500 BC albeit at modern day Dchar Jdid 7.5 miles to the north-east. At its current location, Asilah was established under the Idrisid Dynasty (788–974). In 1471, it was conquered by the Portuguese, who built the well-preserved fortifications seen today. After passing briefly through Moroccan hands in 1589, the town was lost to the Spanish until 1692, when it was again taken by Morocco under the leadership of Alawi Sultan Ismail Ibn Sharif (1645–1727). During the 19th and 20th centuries, Asilah served as a base for Barbary pirates prompting the Austrians to bombard it in 1829. From 1912 until Moroccan independence in 1956, it was part of the Spanish Protectorate.

The sea walls and cemetery at Asilah

Asilah as a visitor destination goes back to 1978, when an annual art and music festival was established. Its success prompted considerable urban renewal. Most visitors today head for the walled Medina, with its whitewashed houses, which provide the perfect canvas for street art during the festival. The best is preserved for posterity.

The walls of the Medina are punctuated by two main gates, Bab el-Houmar facing inland and Bab al-Kasbah facing the port. A rectangular crenellated tower, the Borj al-Qamra, overlooks an open square nearby, where it once served as a residence for the Portuguese king's daughter, who was married to the Portuguese governor of Asilah. The Grand Mosque with its octagonal minaret was built under Sultan Ismail (1645–1727) and occupies the former site of the Kasbah.

The sea walls of the Medina are particularly impressive. Midway along is the former palace of tribal leader Mulai Ahmed er Raisuni (1871–1925), who became governor in 1905. Known to English-speakers as Raisuli, he gained notoriety through the kidnapping of several prominent Westerners (see no. 42). It is said that he tossed convicted murderers from his loggia onto the sea rocks below! The projecting bastion nearby is the Portuguese-built Torre de San Francisco.

The southern end of the sea walls is marked by a bastion variously called Krikia or Caraquia. As well as providing a good vantage point for photographers, it overlooks a projecting stone platform on which is the Sidi Mansour Cemetery. Named after a respected Islamic scholar, who rests here in a domed mausoleum *(marabout)*, it encompasses a set of graves covered in colourful ceramic tiles.

Outside the Medina, in Asilah's New City, the Roman Catholic Church of San Bartolomé can be found. Built in 1925 by Spanish Franciscans, it is one of the few churches in Morocco permitted to ring its bells for Sunday Mass.

Adventurous visitors may like to travel nine miles south-east of Asilah to the village of Chouahed. The extraordinary Mzoura Dolmen found here comprises a group of 176 monoliths surrounding a tumulus. One of the monoliths rises over 17 feet. Dated anywhere between 5,000 and 200 BC, the mound was possibly raised for a local tribal chief. The stones may have acted as a gathering place or ritualistic site. Whatever the date, the site disproves the long-held belief that the Tangier Peninsula during prehistoric times was merely a backdrop to Mediterranean history. Instead, growing evidence suggests the area was populated by a dynamic society that had deeply-held beliefs and was in contact with its neighbours.

Opening Times

Correct at time of going to press but may be subject to change.

Animal Rest Home, New Mountain (California), Route de Boubana north of the Royal Country Club de Tanger, accessible all hours

Borj Dar el-Baroud Interpretation Centre of the Fortifications of Tangier, Medina (Old City), junction of Avenue Mohammed VI and Route de la Plage Merkala (La Corniche), daily 10.00am–4.30pm

Café Hafa, Marshan, Rue Hafa, daily 9.00am–11.00pm

Cape Spartel Lighthouse, Achakkar, Route Agla, daily 8.30am–11.30pm

Cathedral of the Immaculate Conception and the Holy Spirit, Iberia (San Francisco), junction of Rue Sidi Bouabid and Avenue Hassan II, Tue–Sat 10.00am–1.00pm, 6.00–7.15pm, Sun 10.50am–12.15pm

Caves of Hercules, Achakkar, Route des Grottes d'Hercule, daily 10.00am–6.00pm

Central Market (Marché Central), Medina (Old City), Rue Siaghine, daily 8.00am–9.00pm

Cinema Rif & Café, Ville Nouvelle (New City), Grand Socco, Tue–Sun 8.30am–11.00pm

Dar Baroud Hammam, Medina (Old City), 77 Rue Dar Baroud, daily 6.00am–11.00pm

Dar Gnawa, Medina (Old City), Bab el-Marsa, Rue Alkaa, Borj el-Hajoui courtyard lock-up number 2, no fixed opening hours

Dar Niaba Museum (Musée Dar Niaba), Medina (Old City), 41 Rue Siaghine, Wed–Mon 10.00am–6.00pm

Donabo Botanical Gardens, Rmilat, Route du Cap Spartel, Summer (Apr–Sep) Tue–Sun 10.00am–8.00pm, Winter (Oct–Mar) Tue–Sun 10.00am–7.00pm

Fondation pour la Photographie Tanger, Old Mountain, 235 Rue Sidi Masmoudi, Wed–Sun 10.30am–6.00pm

Fondouk Chejra, Ville Nouvelle (New City), Rue Amerique du Sud, daily 9.00am–6.00pm

Galerie Delacroix, Ville Nouvelle (New City), 86 Rue de la Liberté, Tue–Sun 10.00am–1.00pm, 2.30–7.30pm

Gran Café de Paris, Ville Nouvelle (New City), Place de France, daily 6.30am–11.00pm

Grand Mosque (Jami' al-Kebir), Medina (Old City), 76 Rue de la Marine, daily prayers 6.00–6.45am, 1.00–2.30pm, 4.00–5.00pm, 7.00–9.00pm; closed to non-Muslims

Librairie des Colonnes, Ville Nouvelle (New City), 54 Boulevard Pasteur, Mon–Sat 10.00am–8.00pm

Madini, Medina (Old City), 14 Rue Sebou, daily c. 3.00–10.00pm

Mendoubia Palace and Gardens, Ville Nouvelle (New City), off the Grand Socco, daily 8.30am–6.00pm

Moshe Nahon Synagogue, Medina (Old City), Rue Cheikh al Harrak off Rue Synagogues, Sun–Fri 10.00am–5.00pm

Museum of Mediterranean Cultures (Musée des Cultures Méditerranéennes), Medina (Old City), Kasbah, Place de la Kasbah, Tue–Sun 10.00am–6.00pm

Nougat de Tangier, Medina (Old City), junction of Rue Siaghine and Rue Synagogues, daily around midday onwards

Palace of Arts and Culture (Palais des Arts et Culture de Tanger), Malabata, junction of Avenue Mohammed VI and Route Hassania, Mon–Thu 9.00am–5.00pm

Palais des Institutions Italiennes (former Abd al-Hafid Palace), Iberia (San Francisco), Rue Mohamed ben Abdelouahab, Casa d'Italia restaurant Tue–Sun 12.00–3.00pm, 7.00–11.00pm

Phoenician Necropolis, Marshan, Gharsa Ghanam, off Avenue Hadj Mohamed Tazi, open all hours

Port Centre, Ville Nouvelle (New City), Place Bab el-Marsa, Tue–Sun 10.00am–6.00pm

Restaurant Populaire Le Saveur de Poisson, Ville Nouvelle (New City), 2 Escalier Waller, Sat–Thu 1.00–5.00pm, 7.00–10.30pm

St. Andrew's Church, Ville Nouvelle (New City), Rue d'Angleterre, Sat–Thu 10.00am–1.00pm, 3.00–5.00pm

Tangier American Legation Museum, Medina (Old City), 8 Rue d'Amerique (8 Zankat Amerika), Mon–Fri 10.00am–5.00pm, Sat & Sun 10.00am–3.00pm

Villa Harris Museum, Malabata, junction of Boulevard Mohammed VI and Route Hassania, Wed–Mon 10.00am–6.00pm

Villa Perdicaris, Rmilat, Rmilat Park, daily 10.00am–6.00pm; Park daily 7.00am–11.30pm

Further Reading

GUIDEBOOKS

North Africa: The Roman Coast (Ethel Davies), Bradt Travel Guides, 2009

In the Mood for Tanger & Essaouira (Audrey Nait-Challal), Editions In the Mood For, 2025

Moon Morocco (Lucas Peters), Moon Travel, 2023

Tangier and its Surroundings, Assilah & Chefchaouen: An illustrated Guide (Juan Ramón Roca), Roca Vicente-Franqueira, 2011

Lonely Planet Morocco (Helen Ranger et al), Lonely Planet, 2023

Tangier: A Literary Guide for Travellers (Josh Shoemake), I. B. Tauris & Co., 2018

Insight Guide Morocco (Various), Insight Guides, 2017

The Monocle Travel Guide to Marrakech, Tangier & Casablanca (Various), Monocle Travel Guides, 2019

The Rogue's Guide to Tangier (Bert & Mabel Winter), Knockmuldowney Press, 1986

HISTORY

Historia de Tangér (Leopoldo Ceballos López), Almuzara, 2009

A Room with a View: A History of the Grand Hotel Villa de France (Andrew Clandermond & Terence MacCarthy), Minville, 2012

By Royal Appointment: A History of the Continental Hotel (Andrew Clandermond & Terence MacCarthy), Black Eagle Press, 2012

Lord Bute's Palace: A History of the El Minzah (Andrew Clandermond & Terence MacCarthy), Minville, 2012

Beyond the Columns: A History of the Librairie des Colonnes (Andrew Clandermond & Terence MacCarthy), Black Eagle Press, 2013

Portuguese Tangier (1471-1662): Colonial Urban Fabric as Cross-Cultural Skeleton (Martin Malcolm Elbl), Batwolf Press, 2013

Tangier: City of the Dream (Iain Finlayson), Harper Collins, 1992

Tangier: From the Romans to the Rolling Stones (Richard Hamilton), Tauris Parke, 2024

Living Tangier: Migration, Race, and Illegality in a Moroccan City (Abdelmajid Hannoum), University of Pennsylvania Press, 2020

Portrait of Tangier (Rom Landau), Robert Hale, 1952

Morocco: From Empire to Independence (C.R. Pennell), One World Publications, 2009

A Traveller's History of North Africa (Barnaby Rogerson), Duckworth, 2008

Tangier 1661–1684: England's Lost Atlantic Outpost (Enid M.G. Routh), John Murray, 1912

The International City of Tangier (Graham Henry Stuart), Stanford University Press, 1955

Tanger: Realité d'un Mythe (Rachid Tafersiti), Zarouila, 1998

The Sultan's Gift: A History of St. Andrew's Church, Tangier 1881–2006 (Lance Taylor), printed privately, 2005

ART, ARCHITECTURE & GARDENS

Inside Tangier: Houses and Gardens (Nicolò Castellini Baldissera), Vendome Press, 2019

A Dictionary of Painters in Tangier 1669–2003 (Andrew Clandermond & Terence MacCarthy), Lawrence–Arnott Gallery, 2003

Eden Revisited: A Garden in Northern Morocco (Umberto Pasti & Ngoc Minh Ngo), Rizzoli, 2019

The House of a Lifetime: A Collector's Journey in Tangier (Umberto Pasti & Ngoc Minh Ngo), Rizzoli, 2023

TRAVEL MEMOIRS

Travels in Asia and Africa 1325–1354 (Ibn Battuta), Routledge Curzon, 2005

Two Years Beside the Strait (Paul Bowles), Peter Owen, 1990

The Tangier Papers of Samuel Pepys (Ed. Edwin Chappell), Navy Records Society, 1935

For Bread Alone (Mohamed Choukri, trans. Paul Bowles), Telegram Books, 2007

In Tangier (Mohamed Choukri), Telegram Books, 2010

The Tangerine House (Rupert Croft-Cooke), MacMillan, 1956

The Caves of Hercules (Rupert Croft-Cooke), W. H. Allen, 1974

Morocco That Was (Walter Harris), Eland, 1983

The Tangier Diaries: 1962–1979 (John Hopkins), Cadmus Editions, 1998

A Life Full of Holes (Larbi Layachi, trans. Paul Bowles), Grove Press, 1982

Travels with a Tangerine: A Journey in the Footnotes of Ibn Battutah (Tim Mackintosh-Smith), John Murray, 2001

Stories de Tanger (Mohamed Mrabet & Simon-Pierre Hamelin), DU SIROCCO, 2009

Everybody Comes to Dean's: Dean's Bar, Tangier (Francis Poole), Poporo Press, 2009

Tangier: A Writer's Notebook (Angus Stewart), Hutchinson, 1977

The Pillars of Hercules: A Grand Tour of the Mediterranean (Paul Theroux), Ballantine Books, 1996

The Odyssey of Ibn Battuta (David Waines), I. B. Tauris, 2012

In Morocco (Edith Wharton), Charles Scribner, 1920

LITERATURE & BIOGRAPHY

Gates to Tangier (Mois Benarroch), Lulu.com, 2019

Interzone (William S. Burroughs), Penguin Publishing Group, 1990

Naked Lunch (William S. Burroughs), Grove Press, 1992

The Sheltering Sky (Paul Bowles), John Lehmann, 1949

Let It Come Down (Paul Bowles), John Lehmann, 1952

Paul Bowles: A Life (Virginia Spencer Carr), Peter Owen, 2005

Tales of Tangier: The Complete Short Stories (Mohamed Choukri), Yale University Press, 2023

El Raisuni: The Sultan of the Mountains (Rosita Forbes), Thornton Butterworth, 1924

The Dream at the End of the World: Paul Bowles and the Literary Renegades in Tangier (Michelle Green), Harper Collins, 1991

Love with a Few Hairs (Mohamed Mrabet, trans. Paul Bowles), Arena, 1986

Colonial Affairs: Bowles, Burroughs and Chester Write Tangier (Greg A. Mullins), University of Wisconsin Press, 2002

Shadows and Light: The Extraordinary Life of James McBey (Alasdair Soussi), Scotland Street Press, 2022

Stars in the Firmament: Tangier Characters 1660-1960 (David S. Woolman), Passeggiata Press, 1997

FOOD AND DRINK

Flavours of Morocco: Delicious Recipes from North Africa (Ghillie Başan), Ryland, Peters & Small, 2008

Tagines: Explore the Traditional Tastes of North Africa (Ghillie Başan), Aquamarine, 2014

The Modern Tagine Cookbook (Ghillie Başan), Ryland, Peters & Small, 2019

Moroccan Tea: Easy to Prepare (Morocco Cultures), Independently Published, 2020

Couscous and Other Good Food from Morocco (Paula Wolfert), Harper Collins, 1973

ILLUSTRATED BOOKS

Tanger Entre Orient et Occident (Philip Abensur), Editions Sutton, 2009

Spirits of Tangier (Tessa Codrington), Arcadia Books Ltd., 2008

Tanger: Porte Entre Deux Mondes (Jean-Louis Miège & Georges Bousquet), ACR Édition, 1992

Tanger International (Paul Servant), Committee of Propaganda & Tourism of the International Administration of the Tangier Zone, 1929

WEBSITES

www.visittanger.com/en/

www.tanger-experience.com

www.discoveringtangier.wordpress.com

Acknowledgements

This book is dedicated to my mother, Mary, who made possible my first visit to Tangier in the early 1970s, and to my late father, Trevor, who loved Tangier. He inspired me to track down things unique, hidden, and unusual in the first place.

For kind permission to take photographs, as well as for arranging access and the provision of information, the following people are most gratefully acknowledged:

Abdelghani Aouf (Café Baba), Moncef Bouali (Librairie des Colonnes), Ben Boubker Abdelilah (Café Porto Rico), Baroudi Mohammad Badri, Yto Barrada (The Mothership), Paul Belvoir (Donabo Botanical Gardens), Bernard Bernatzik, Souleiman Berrada (Fondation pour la Photographie Tanger), Cathedral of the Immaculate Conception and the Holy Spirit, Ahmed Chliah (Jabal Rif de Tanja), Stéphanie Gaou (Les Insolites Bookshop), Abdellah El Gourd (Dar Gnawa), Sean Gullette, Elisabeth-Joe Harriet, Abdul Latif Kasabji, Daniel Kennedy, Yassin Khamlichi (St. Andrew's Church), Douae La Hrir (Dar al-Drazz), Younes Hariri Madini (Madini), Raihab Maknassi (Fendak Dar Dbagh), Paul May, Omar Menissar, Moshe Nahon Synagogue, Audrey Nait-Challal, and Jonas Senhadji, Adil Daaji and Tima Zarouki (Interzone).

Special thanks to Margaret Bald, Richard Hamilton, Jordi Mas, Lucas Peters, Josh Shoemake, and Alasdair Soussi for sharing with me their own invaluable knowledge and experiences of Tangier. Also, to my friend in Vienna, John Carchrae, for expending his valuable time and energy in so expertly proof-reading my manuscript and making the necessary corrections and amendments.

Thanks also to my brother Adrian and great cousin James Dickinson for bringing interesting news items to my attention, my old friend Simon Laffoley for his expert help with the photos, Igor Brejc at Scalable Maps, and Digital Bits for managing my website.

Finally, heartfelt thanks to my wife, Roswitha, for her tireless support of my work and wonderful company on field trips.

Imprint

1st Edition published by The Urban Explorer, 2025
A division of Duncan J. D. Smith
contact@duncanjdsmith.com
www.onlyinguides.com
www.duncanjdsmith.com

Original graphic design: Stefan Fuhrer
Typesetting and picture editing: Luke Griffin/Griffix Design
Map design: wwwscalablemaps.com
Map data: © OpenStreetMap contributors
Printed and bound in Dubai by Oriental Press

All papers used by The Urban Explorer are natural, recyclable products made from wood grown in sustainable, well-managed forests.

ISBN 978-3-9505392-6-4

An electricity meter box adorned by street artist Punksy (see no. 22)